THE MONDAY CONNECTION

THE MONDAY CONNECTION

A Spirituality of Competence,
Affirmation, and Support
in the Workplace

William E. Diehl

HarperSanFrancisco
A Division of HarperCollins*Publishers*

FIRST EDITION

Library of Congress Cataloging-in-Publication Data

Diehl, William E.
    The Monday Connection : a spirituality of competence, affirmation, and support
in the workplace/William E. Diehl.—1st ed.
        p.   cm.
        ISBN 0-06-061925-2 (alk. paper)
        1. Work—Religious aspects—Christianity.   2. Christian life—1960–
I. Title.
        BT738.5.D56 1991
        248.8'8—dc20   90-55292
                                                                                            CIP

---

91 92 93 94 95 RRD(H) 10 9 8 7 6 5 4 3 2 1

This edition is printed on acid-free paper that meets the American National Standards Institute Z39.48 Standard.

To Judy

CONTENTS

Introduction

In today's world "Sunday Christians" are irrelevant. The hymns, sermons, prayers, and creeds of Sunday morning have no impact upon the outside world unless they shape the lives of Christians during the rest of the week. The false idols and pernicious values of society remain unchallenged unless "Monday Christians" act and witness to their faith in everyday life in a relevant manner.

Yet most Christians are unable to bring into the experiences of everyday life the basic elements of the faith they profess on a Sunday morning. When asked how the experiences of 11:00 A.M. on Monday connect with what they experienced at 11:00 A.M. on Sunday, in church, most Christians are at a total loss for words.

Having led conferences and seminars with laypeople on faith and life themes for more than twenty-five years, I feel confident in making such statements. Recent studies done by the Gallup organization, Search Institute, and others have solidly confirmed my observations.

For the majority of churchgoing people, Sunday morning is the time to get away from the cares of the world and to think about "spiritual" things. Sunday worship is a refuge from the world. When pressed to explain how the Sunday experience relates to their daily lives, people frequently respond that they gain strength for the rest of the week. When asked how the strength shows up in their daily lives, however, they become vague. They try to be more patient, more friendly, they say. They try to be more ethical. But when asked if they experience God's presence in their daily activities, the answer is almost universally, "No." They find no spirituality in daily life.

The ministry of the laity is an issue that seems to ebb and flow within the program priorities of most American denominations. All Christian churches support the principle of a ministry of all God's people, yet few have real insight into how to implement the principle. The corporate culture of churches, like the cultures of all our corporate organizations, looks inward rather than outward. We believe that we serve the church by serving in its structures, not in the structures outside the church. Consequently, few national or local church bodies affirm, equip, and support their members for ministry in the world.

A paradox of major proportions is surfacing in American society in the 1990s. On the one hand, large numbers of people are experiencing a spiritual awakening. Many are intensely searching for meaning in life. The Gallup polls tell us that in the past ten years, the number of Americans who believe that Jesus Christ is the Son of God has increased from 78 percent to 84 percent. The number who claim a solid commitment to Christ has increased from 60 percent to 66 percent.[1]

Yet, during that same ten-year period, the number of unchurched Americans rose from 41 percent to 44 percent. The mainline denominations have experienced staggering membership losses, in some cases as high as 25 percent in the past two decades.[2] Moreover, the age of those who remain church members is significantly above the average for all Americans, which does not bode well for the future. And Gallup also reports that the largest criticism of religious institutions is coming from those who are still church members: 58 percent say that religious institutions are too much concerned with organizational matters.

To blame this paradox on the excessive "privatization" of religion in America is to point to the symptoms while ignoring the disease. The real problem is that our churches are failing to lead people into the experience of faith. What does it profit a person to worship God for one hour in a church on Sunday but be unable to experience God's presence in the Monday world?

The mission of the church is to transform lives; its failure to do so in recent years can be measured by its own body count. The rhetoric of the church is a call for all its members to serve God in their daily lives; the reality is that there is a huge wall separating people's Sunday experience from their Monday experience.

I have spent most of my life working in business and industry, and have at the same time remained a loyal member of my church. For much of this time I found it difficult to make the connections between Sunday and Monday. Sadly, my church offered virtually no help. I have had to claim my own ministry in daily life and discover for myself how to make the "Monday connection." Even today I am called a "dedicated layperson" solely because of my work in my congregation and my denomination. My church has yet to call me a "dedicated layperson" for my efforts to bring God's presence into my daily work, my relationships with others, my ethical decision making and my values. In fact, because I have tried to call my church to its transforming mission, some have seen me as disloyal and anticlerical.

I have written this book to share the ways in which I have been able to connect my confessed faith of Sunday with my operational faith of Monday. In these chapters we will explore five types of Christian ministry in daily life: the ministries of competency, presence, ethics, change, and values. Although others may order their faith-life relationships differently, these are the ways that make sense to me and to the people with whom I have worked.

I write primarily for the many church members who believe in God and who miss the experience of God in their daily lives. For those church leaders who are interested in the ministries of all the people of God, I will share ways in which the church can affirm, equip, and support laypeople in their daily lives. But the current interest in spirituality and the increased search for meaning on the part of many Americans has prompted me to give Christians information that—with or without the help of the institutional church—will enable them to connect faith and daily life.

The Holy Spirit will not abandon those who truly seek to make their Monday connection. I can bear witness to this fact in my own life.

I

THE
SUNDAY/MONDAY
GAP

CHAPTER 1

Unconnected

"I can't understand it," he said. "I firmly believe religion should be important in everyone's life . . . and yet, when I go to church, it leaves me absolutely cold." The conversation took place at dinner with the chief executive officer of one of the Fortune 500 companies.

He continued, "Our church is less than half full for Sunday worship, the liturgy is out of the Middle Ages, the sermons seldom relate to what is going on in my life, and the people look bored and unhappy."

"Well, then, what keeps you going back to church?" I asked.

"Actually, I attend church less often than I did ten years ago," he replied. "But I continue to believe that religion is important. I believe in God. I desperately want my grandchildren to get a good religious training. Yet what goes on at our church on Sunday seems so irrelevant to the rest of my life."

He shook his head. "It's a weird situation. It really is."

My dinner companion is not alone. His "weird situation" is rather common among Americans and is apparently becoming more so.

In fall 1988 the Gallup organization released the results of a ten-year study on churchgoing in America.[1] The Gallup people discovered that from 1978 to 1988 the percentage of unchurched American adults had risen from 41 percent to 44 percent. Based on the Bureau of Labor Statistics' population estimate, this drop of 3 percent equates to 7 million more unchurched Americans during that ten-year period.

The most striking discovery in the study was that while church membership is steadily shrinking, an increasing number of adults

7

believe in Jesus Christ as the Son of God. The number of Americans who affirm that conviction rose from 78 percent in 1978 to 84 percent in 1988. Significantly more Americans are expressing religious convictions, while fewer are staying in the churches.

As my friend said, "It's a weird situation."

Evidence in support of Gallup's findings can be found everywhere.

In the 1970s alone the United Presbyterian Church reported a 19 percent loss of members. In the same period the Disciples of Christ were down 17 percent, the Episcopalians 15 percent, the United Church of Christ 11 percent, and the United Methodist Church had 9 percent fewer members.[2]

On the other hand, the more conservative and fundamentalist churches have been experiencing significant growth. We will look at the reasons for this in later chapters.

Not only is membership declining in the mainline denominations, but church attendance is also. Even the Roman Catholic church, which has been able to increase membership, is struggling with decreased attendance. From 1958 to 1982 the number of Roman Catholics attending weekly mass dropped from 74 percent to 51 percent.[3] In Detroit, for example, the diocese announced in December 1988 that forty-six churches would be closed due to inadequate membership support.

We have every evidence that the situation will get worse. A visitor to a typical congregation on any given Sunday morning will see a disproportionately high percentage of silver-haired worshipers. Although 40 percent of all Americans are between eighteen and thirty-four, 41 percent of all Methodists and 42 percent of all Disciples of Christ are fifty-five or older. The mean age of United Church of Christ members is fifty-five.[4]

Furthermore, of those fewer and older Americans who are still attending churches, a disproportionately high percentage are women. My dinner companion was, in fact, rather typical of American males today.

MY STORY

I believe my own experience can shed light on what is going on with respect to religion in America today.

I was baptized in a Lutheran church and was dutifully enrolled by my mother in every program our congregation had to offer the young. Kindergarten, Sunday school, weekday church school, vacation church school, catechetical classes, youth league—I got the whole truckload. I was also enrolled in the children's choir, much against my will. Not only was I a poor singer, but I detested being dressed up in a white choir robe with a silly black bow tie tucked under my chin. I finally managed to escape the children's choir, only to appear as an acolyte in another white robe with an even larger floppy bow tie. How I hoped that none of my classmates from junior high school would see me in that stupid outfit! But it was repeatedly pointed out to me that I was serving God by doing these things.

I suffered through countless church services in which the music was dreary, the sermons were totally beyond my comprehension, and the people looked like a rather unhappy lot, except for those who were asleep. But not one shred of what I experienced in church had any relationship to the experiences of my life.

My grandparents on both sides of the family were regular churchgoers, but I never saw how it made any difference in their daily lives. Not once did I see any of my parents or grandparents pray outside of a church service. At mealtimes it was always "Billy" who was expected to recite his little prayer. A parent would usually say my bedtime prayer with me when I was very young, but I have no idea if they prayed before their own bedtime. We never discussed religion at our dinner table. It seemed to me that my parents' and grandparents' religious experience was confined to what went on in church on Sunday morning.

When I was old enough to break away from the family, churchgoing was one of the first things I discarded. Religion was for the birds. Church was phony. I completely left the church, and sometimes proudly boasted to my friends that I did not believe in God. In retrospect I think I may have had my fingers crossed on that boast; but I certainly had no use for the church. It related in no way to my daily life.

During World War II, I was a combat medic in Europe with the 11th Tank Battalion of the 10th Armored Division. The first wounded person I ever pulled out of a burning tank was one of my best friends. His left leg was completely gone beneath the knee. I lived with fear, pain, and death for weeks on end, and on more than one occasion I cried out to God for help. Toward the end of the war, our tank battalion liberated several prisoner of war camps and one concentration camp. I was shocked by how brutal human beings could be to each other.

I returned home a very sober person as a result of these traumatic experiences. And I could not forget how, in my moments of deepest need, I had turned to God in prayer. I decided to go back to my church once more.

Unfortunately, nothing had changed. The music was still dreary, the sermons had no relationship to my life experiences, and the people still looked unhappy.

The next few years were largely taken up with completing college, marrying Judy, getting a good job, and becoming a father. After completing my training with Bethlehem Steel Corporation, I was assigned as a salesperson in our Detroit district sales office. Judy and I settled into a tiny duplex house with our two babies, six hundred miles away from home and friends.

Joining a church seemed to be the right thing to do. We could make new friends and give our children a religious education. The church we joined in Detroit was, in many ways, better than the one we left behind. People were open and friendly, the worship services were more lively, and the pastor had a deep commitment to the faith. We met other young families and developed strong bonds, which still exist some thirty years later and hundreds of miles apart. We served God by teaching the high school class, by being youth group advisers, by being on the church council. Judy sang in the choir (it was obvious to all that God was not well-served by my singing). Judy and I were frequently praised for our dedicated service to the church, and I was even given a special award for being such a "dedicated layperson." It was all very nice and cozy—in our church.

No Connections

But there was a problem, a major problem: My Sunday experience had no connection to my Monday world. The words that came to me from the Bible and the pulpit made no sense to me in my weekday world.

"So, the last will be first and the first last," Jesus said to his followers (Matthew 20:16 RSV). Yet I was out there trying to get orders for Bethlehem Steel and competing with other very aggressive salespeople. Should I, as a Christian, really let the others get ahead of me? I wouldn't have my job very long if I did.

In response to a question as to how often his followers should forgive someone, Jesus replied, "Seventy times seven" (Matthew 18:22b RSV). Well, I happened to have a customer who was very slow in paying his bills, and my home office credit department recommended that we cut off shipments to him. I argued that we should be patient with the customer and give him another chance. The credit manager asked how long I felt we should keep this up. Should I have said, "Seventy times seven"? *That* would have made the rounds of conversation among home office management!

In the course of my sales work, I developed friendships with customers who were very wealthy. For the first time in my life, I found myself playing golf with the country club set and eating lunches at exclusive city clubs. On the one hand, I heard many Sunday morning warnings about the love of money being an evil and, on the other hand, there was that parable in which Jesus encouraged his followers to "make friends for yourselves with worldly wealth, so that when it gives out, you will be welcomed in the eternal home" (Luke 16:9 TEV). Well, which was it? Should I distance myself from the wealthy or make friends of them?

From the Bible and from the pulpit, I heard the orders to be "witnesses" for Christ in the world. How? What did that mean? Do I tell my coworkers about the pastor's sermon? Do I hand out leaflets on street corners? And, in particular, how in the world do I witness to a gospel of grace in a world of works? How does the doctrine of unmerited grace get communicated in a world where everything is based on merit?

On Sunday we were admonished to "let your light so shine," that others would know we were Christians (Matthew 5:16 RSV). What did that mean for me? In the workplace no one ever talked about religion. It was absolutely not done. There was no way that I could possibly tell which of my associates were Christians and which were not. We dressed the same, shared similar values, had similar concerns, and lived similar lives. I didn't see any Christian light shining and I knew mine wasn't either.

Since I was a member of a Lutheran congregation, there were frequent references to Luther's affirmation of the universal priesthood of the baptized. We were all to serve as the intermediaries between God and other humans. Yet I saw absolutely no way in which I served as a priest in my Monday world.

Other messages, however, came through quite clearly. If I was unable to make a committee meeting at our church because of a business commitment, I was made to feel that a "true" believer would not give a work-related engagement a higher priority than a church meeting. The pastor frequently used businesspeople as examples whenever he needed a sermon illustration of evil in our world. Within the Christian community, then, I was certainly not eager to admit that I was in business.

The gap between the rhetoric of what the church was saying on Sunday and the reality of what was happening in my life on Monday was enormous. The problem was that my church was speaking as an extrovert, but behaving as an introvert. It was calling on me to serve as a disciple of Christ in the world without giving me any help on how to do it. On the other hand, I got help in the form of affirmation, training, and even prayers for my service in the church as a Sunday school teacher, youth adviser, and church council member. For my Monday work as a Christian businessperson in a highly competitive environment, however, I received no affirmation, no training, no support, and no prayers. Nothing. There was absolutely no connection between Sunday and Monday.

For a number of years I accepted the fact that I lived in two worlds, the Sunday world of religion and the Monday world of secularism. I was not greatly troubled in my Monday world over my inability to relate my faith to the experiences in my life; the disturbance began to show up more and more in my Sunday world. I became increasingly uneasy about the hypocrisy of a church that preached Christian service in the world, but practiced Christian service exclusively within its own institution.

Something had to change. Either I had to admit to the hypocrisy of my Sunday world and leave the church again, or I had to find a way to bridge those two worlds in my own life. The option of leaving the church was not acceptable to me. My faith in God had become solid. The ministry of word and sacrament of the church was an important part of my pilgrimage of faith, even though I did not see how it connected with my Monday world. My life within the church had become too warm and cozy for me to leave it. Moreover, I was convinced that the rhetoric of the church was *right*. I did believe that all God's people were called into a universal priesthood at the time of their baptism.

I also believed that being a businessperson and being a Christian were not incompatible. I believed that all of creation was in God's concern. "The earth is the Lord's and the fulness thereof, the world and those who dwell therein," wrote the Psalmist (Psalm 24:1 RSV). Not just certain parts of it; all of it. "For God so loved the world that he gave his only Son," begins that golden verse of the New Testament (John 3:16 RSV). It doesn't say, "For God so loved the church." It was for the world. All of it. Even my world of business.

My choice was clear: to stay in the church and try to work out the connections between Sunday and Monday by myself. But in accepting that choice I would have to deal with the hypocrisy of an institution that said one thing and practiced something else. I would have to speak out about the lack of a Monday connection and try to help the church find ways to deal with that problem.

Discovering Ministry in Daily Life

Since my church was in no way helping me to claim and carry out my ministry in daily life, I had to find another source. I found that source in books.

First came Elton Trueblood, a remarkable Quaker writer. In the first years of our marriage, Judy and I came to know Martin and Margie Trueblood, Elton's son and daughter-in-law. Because of them I bought *The Common Ventures of Life*. It was a gentle book, but just right for the start of my pilgrimage. It led me to see that the common events of life, such as birth, marriage, work, and death, have deep spiritual significance.

More books followed in quick order: *The Recovery of Family Life, Alternative to Futility, Signs of Hope,* and others broadened my view beyond that of my church. *Your Other Vocation* began my exploration into my ministry in my job. *The Company of the Committed* encouraged me to initiate the formation of our first small support group, which met in homes to discuss faith-life issues. The nineteen Elton Trueblood books I read have a special place in my library and my heart.[5]

Somewhere along the way Mark Gibbs broke into my life. Unlike Trueblood's first book, which was gentle, Mark Gibbs's first book, *God's Frozen People,* went off like a Roman candle.[6] It sent sparks in all directions, and opened the way for me to begin to see what the church can and cannot do to support ministry in daily life. The sequel, *God's Lively People,* further expanded my vision as to what I needed to do to claim my ministry.[7]

I found many other books along the way. Authors like Elizabeth O'Conner, Peter Berger, C. S. Lewis, John Robinson, William Stringfellow, John Howard Yoder, and many others literally sprung the gates wide open for me to engage in my own ministries in daily life. I was driven by them to read theology by Niebuhr, Tillich, Barth, Bultman, Kierkegaard, Luther, Bonhoeffer, and others.

Reflecting on those years of growth through books, I note that none of them, not one, came to my attention through my pastor or anyone in my congregation. I had to discover them on my own.

At the same time, however, I was also experiencing some growth through my involvement with the church. Worship services did become more meaningful. The confession and absolution that comes with Holy Communion was important in keeping me going when I knew that at so many points I was failing in my ministries. Through sermons and study programs, I became more knowledgeable about the Bible. My emotions were touched by church music. I learned to experience *koinonia,* Christian community, through small groups within the church. Conversations with church theologians were helpful (most of the time) in clarifying my readings in theology.

Looking back on those years of searching for my own ministries, I must acknowledge an important point: My reading of books and my involvement with small groups of Christians in discussion and debate were far more influential in my discovery of ministry than were the congregations to which we belonged and the denomination in which I served.

THE DISCONNECTED CHURCH

The decline in membership of American churches has been most evident among the mainline Protestant denominations, which have experienced actual membership decreases. Other denominations, such as the Roman Catholic church and the Southern Baptist Convention, have experienced some membership growth, but have failed to keep up with the growth in the US population. The real growth in church membership has taken place within what Martin Marty calls the "evangelical-moralist" sector of American religion. Many observers credit this fact to America's greater focus on individualism.

During the 1980s individualism was a hot topic among many social commentators. The turbulent 1960s and 1970s caused many Americans to have less faith in the ability of their institutions to shape society. The Reagan years fed the fires of individualism and painted public institutions as the cause of rather than the solution to many of society's problems. The churches, too, fell victim to a diminished public respect for institutions.

There was a time, not too many years ago, when the nation's major weekly news magazines had a regular section devoted to religion. No longer. Religious news today generally centers around activities, good or bad, of religious leaders, not their institutions.

Martin Marty has pointed out that while the influence of mainline Protestant denominations has declined in our society, the evangelical-moralist sector of American religion has gained access to the White House, the Supreme Court, and the Congress. "It has a near-monopoly on mass media religion news, popular religion, and the production of religious celebrities."[8] Marty states that the evangelical-moralists have arrived where their grandparents were often reluctant to go. "Religion, for an older generation, was about evangelism and saving souls, not moralizing in the public sphere," he adds.

The mainline denominations have attempted to gain access to the White House, the Supreme Court, and the Congress through institutional means, such as social statements, offices for governmental affairs, pronouncements of bishops, and actions of church legislative assemblies. The evangelical-moralists, on the other hand, have done it through individuals who have been supported by members of their churches. It is clear that the mainline denominations, which are losing membership, tend to relate to society through institutional actions; the more fundamentalist denominations, which are gaining members, tend to relate to society through the actions of individual members. That distinction is crucial to the message of this book.

Much has been said and written in recent years about this country's excessive attention to individualism. Individualism is a fundamental part of American identity. Our founding documents grant all citizens important individual rights and protections. Individualism has deep roots in American society.

Nonetheless, as Robert Bellah and his associates point out in *Habits of the Heart*, excessive individualism can be destructive to any society.[9] Leaders of mainline Protestant denominations have lauded the findings of *Habits of the Heart* and have frequently quoted them when trying to explain membership losses. "Excessive religious individualism has diminished membership in our churches," goes the explanation. To prove this conviction the mainliners point to membership growth in those conservative denominations that focus entirely on individual salvation. "They teach 'me and Jesus' without regard to the rest of God's creation," goes the criticism. There has been some truth in such charges, but recent developments within the evangelical communities of faith suggest that an important aspect of religious individualism cries out for nourishment: experiencing faith in daily life.

Jesus' commandment to love one another raises an interesting question for today's Christians. Do I express my love for others through support of a religious institution that does ministry in the world, or do I express my love for others through individual acts in my daily life? Most church leaders would say that it is both, and probably most American Christians would agree. But what seems to have developed among many American Christians is a real disenchantment with church leadership that concentrates almost exclusively on institutional issues and ignores the nurturing of members in their individual experiences of faith.

The Gallup study on the "unchurched American" provides valuable data on this matter. The report says, "Religious institutions get decidedly worse grades today than they did a decade ago, and the biggest increase in criticism came from the churched." For example, "In 1978, 47 percent of the churched said most churches and synagogues are too concerned with organizational issues; in 1988 this rose to 58 percent."[10] This growing criticism comes not from the ranks of those who have already left the church; it comes from those who have stayed behind as loyal members.

Bellah and his associates point out that church members identify their faith primarily with what goes on in their personal lives and in their local parish. They are much less influenced religiously by the pronouncements of bishops or "religious specialists beyond the local parish ministry."[11]

TWO TYPES OF INDIVIDUALISM

Two types of religious individualism appear in the Gallup study and similar writings. The first type says that a person can be a good Christian or Jew without attending a church or synagogue. The Gallup report finds that 76 percent of all Americans agree with that statement.[12] This response is virtually the same as the 78 percent who agreed in 1978. Eighty percent of all Americans believe that "one should arrive at his or her religious beliefs independent of any church or synagogue."[13] In 1978 the response was 81 percent. It is this type of individualism that the churches rightly need to combat, because it implies that God does not work through institutions. How are religious beliefs shaped and passed along from one generation to another without the benefit of religious institutions? Where do we go to learn of religious beliefs if there are no institutions? Churches and synagogues are absolutely essential for the maintenance of a religious faith.

The second kind of religious individualism is different. It has to do with how an individual experiences his or her faith. Religious faith involves more than accepting a set of principles. Religious principles are meaningless unless they shape the actions of our lives. For example, it is pointless to believe that one should pray if one never actually prays. The theologian, Paul Tillich, maintains, "There is no faith without participation!"[14] In *Hunger for Experience: Vital Religious Communities in America,* John E. Biersdorf concludes that, "People today hunger for the experience of reality out of which life's meaning may come, not for a *discussion* of reality."[15]

The Gallup study surfaces this second type of religious individualism. What does it mean when 58 percent of church members claim that most churches and synagogues are too concerned with organizational issues? Too concerned? As compared to what? What other issues can there possibly be in a local congregation apart from organizational issues? Individual issues, that's what. Issues of what is going on in my daily life and how God relates to them. Issues of how my Sunday experience in church relates to my weekday experiences in the world.

EXPERIENCING FAITH

It is my conviction that the church's failure to nurture this second type of experiential individualism is responsible for the first type of institutional individualism that says one does not *need* to be a church or synagogue member to be a good Christian or Jew.

Biersdorf's study confirms this connection. He concludes that the conservative or evangelical denominations have grown because they have tapped into the need for people to experience their faith. Where this need has been neglected, as it has been in most mainline denominations, Biersdorf finds "institutional distress."[16] I agree. Churches that encourage people to experience their faith are alive and growing; churches that neglect this aspect are dying.

Dr. Haskell M. Miller, of Wesley Theological Seminary in Washington, supports this opinion. It is his conviction that the most significant factor in membership loss in the mainline denominations is the difficulty that increasing numbers of people have in reconciling the teachings of their religious traditions with their ongoing social and cultural experiences. Dr. Miller says that while "faith-shattering" changes have taken place in the lives of church members, the church often is seen as irrelevant. "As a result," he says, "a conviction is growing that the distance between the new realities and the stance of the church is unbridgeable." While some members are dropping out, others "are suppressing their misgivings and maintaining a stance of determined loyalty, though with little enthusiasm or fervor."[17]

In a report prepared for the Religious Education Association of the United States and Canada, Dr. Constance Leean studied faith development among adults. She discovered that most people do not equate faith with a set of beliefs or dogmas, but see it as more experiential. She urges churches to provide opportunities for "discussion of personal faith experiences." The concluding recommendations take dead aim at those church leaders who condemn all types of religious individualism. "Rather than be dismayed over the growing personalization of religion," she writes, "religious communities ought to align themselves with people's spiritual quests and complement this 'seeking' by offering an historical, theological, and communal context for such explorations."[18]

In a speech to the board of Religion in American Life in 1988, George Gallup stated that his survey's finding that nearly half of all Americans can point to religious experiences in their lives is "one of the most significant survey findings ever uncovered."[19] He concludes that the decade of the 1990s could be an important time of renewal and deepened religious commitment among Americans if the churches affirm, equip, and support their laity in their daily lives.

CONCERNS OF CHURCH LEADERS

Pastors occasionally express the concern that, "If my people engage in ministry in the world, who will be around to help me in the work of the congregation?" The Priorities Task Force of the Presbyterian Church (USA) expressed a similar concern in a report to its 1988 General Assembly Council. Among its predictions was the warning that the ministry of the laity will be oriented to the arenas of daily work instead of to "churchcraft."

> This results in the decrease of traditional "volunteers" for church life, loss of vision of the church as "the body of Christ," increased pressure upon the clergy to be the professional minister, slow erosion of "Christian" perspective and values through accommodation to the values of society in the workplace and isolation from the larger "Christian" community.[20]

The entire list of predictions is defeatist and negative. It is a sad illustration of how utterly out of touch is the leadership of some of the mainline Protestant denominations.

For those pastors who express concern about loss of support in their parish, I have good news. The reverse of their fears is the reality of what happens.

I know of no persons who think that their Christian call is to do ministry in and to the world who are not also vital, active, contributing members of their congregations. Why? Because it is within the community of faith gathered for word and sacrament, learning and affirmation, that the people of God can receive the support necessary to do Christian ministry in their places of work, family, and community.

For almost twenty years I have been conducting conferences and retreats for congregations of most of the major American Christian denominations. I have never found a congregation that was sincerely committed to helping equip its people for ministry in daily life that was not a vital, active, purposeful, and growing community of faith. Not a single one. Not in twenty years.

If those denominations that are losing members do not wake up to the fact that this loss is occurring *because* they are not nourishing their members for ministry in daily life, the dreary predictions of the Presbyterians' Priority Task Force will surely come true.

SQUANDERING POTENTIAL

It is unfortunate that the mainline denominations have been losing membership. But what is even more unfortunate is that many denominations and their congregations are squandering opportunities to extend the witness of the Christian faith into the world through the millions of members who are still loyal to their institutions.

The authors of *Habits of the Heart* report in great detail an interview with Father Paul Morrison, rector of St. Stephen's Episcopal Church in the San Francisco Bay Area. The congregation has quite a few active parish outreach programs, such as visitations to shut-ins and the sick, and a number of members are active in a local mission that feeds, clothes, and houses the hungry and homeless. Father Morrison noted, however, that the major criticism he received from a parish evaluation was that he was too quick to assume that Christian commitment meant working in the parish. His members asked that they be supported where they are in the world. He said he discovered that he had "strong laypeople working in banks, in corporations, or at the university where they find it is very difficult to live out the Christian life, and they're very lonely and they mustn't be."[21] He added that "politics, law, and other professions," often looked down on by the church, are potential areas of Christian service. Morrison believes church people must be helped to fulfill "their vocations and calling and ministry effectively and nobly in those areas."[22]

The interviewers observed that the Episcopal church has traditionally stood close to the centers of power in our country and asked if the potential is still there for the church, through its members, to influence American power structures from within. His reply was,

> If we recover to any extent our support of our people in their vocations and ministries in the world, then maybe one would have enough confidence to say yes, from the inside we certainly can take responsibility, because our best people are there and they are nourished and succored by the church and ready to do the job. Right now it seems almost accidental if there is any relationship between Episcopalians in power and the Gospel.[23]

"It seems accidental if there is any relationship between Episcopalians in power and the Gospel." This is a damning indictment of all mainline churches, for the statement is universally applicable. It is true in the life of the chief executive officer whose story was presented at the start of this chapter. It has been true through much of my life. I know from years of experience that it is true in the lives of millions of faithful Christians in America today.

Dr. George Gallup, Jr., in analyzing the findings of "The Unchurched American, 1988," states that there is still time for the churches to make a comeback in the 1990s, "but there are some giant 'ifs.' " The first "if": "If churches and synagogues listen and respond to the remarkable spiritual breakthroughs people experience and help people build upon these experiences." The second "if" is "to give people the essential tools with which to build their faith." Gallup feels that churches need to emphasize the practical "how-to" aspects of connecting faith and daily life. Third, citing evidence that Americans are clearly "biblical illiterates," Gallup insists that churches must encourage people to make a commitment to reading and studying the Bible. The fourth "if" for church renewal is if churches target certain groups in the population: "those in business and the professions—businessmen, doctors, lawyers, and others who must constantly make ethical judgments, sometimes life-or-death decisions. These people are in great need of spiritual nourishment, but often are not receiving it."[24]

In the following chapters we will consider the kinds of ministries laypeople can claim as their own. Woven into these chapters are examples of how American churches can carry out the "ifs" of Dr. Gallup's challenge.

Because the American churches appear to be so totally unaware of the lack of a Monday connection in the lives of their members, laypeople need to help each other discern and develop their ministries in daily life. But we also have an obligation to try to help our church institutions come to grips with their own lack of connection. For the sake of the world, for the sake of the gospel, we must find these ways.

II

COMPETENCY

CHAPTER 2

Just Doing My Job

At approximately 2:00 A.M. on Friday, February 24, 1989, United Airlines Flight 811 took off from Honolulu, Hawaii, destined for New Zealand. The Boeing 747 jumbo jet was climbing through an altitude of 22,000 feet, when suddenly there was a violent shudder of the fuselage. A loud crash followed, and the huge plane leaned to the left. The cockpit crew was unaware at the time that the forward cargo door of the jet had been blown open, tearing a huge 10-foot by 25-foot hole in the side of the plane. Nine passengers were sucked out of the plane to their deaths.

The pilot, Captain David Cronin, observed immediately that the two right engines had been damaged by the flying debris and had ceased to function. The crew reached for their oxygen masks only to discover that they were not working. A quick check of the cabin revealed the presence of the huge hole. Captain Cronin immediately put the plane into a sharp descent to gain more oxygen. But, because he did not want to increase the size of the hole in the fuselage, he decided not to do the recommended power dive and opted for a somewhat slower descent. He headed back to Hawaii, a hundred miles away.

Captain Cronin, a veteran of thirty-eight years of military and commercial flying, put all his knowledge and experience on the line. To compensate for the lack of thrust from the two right engines, he struggled to hold the control column steady with his hands while using his feet to put pressure on the control floor rudder to stabilize the plane.

His stickiest problem, however, was deciding how fast to fly. Captain Cronin slowed the plane as close to the stall speed as possible to keep the air rushing over the plane from further widening the hole in the fuselage. Because the hole had changed the aerodynamics of the huge craft, the usual data regarding stall speed was no longer relevant. The pilot had to use his best judgment.

Furthermore, since the plane had just taken on 300,000 pounds of fuel for the long flight, it was too heavy to land without collapsing the landing gear. Captain Cronin began dumping fuel at the maximum rate, but quickly calculated that he would still be above the recommended weight for landing unless he circled the island. Fearing that the hole in the fuselage might widen, he decided to risk landing overweight.

But then he encountered a new problem. The wing flaps used to slow down the plane were not working properly. He would have to land the plane at a higher than recommended speed.

Captain Cronin headed the plane for the longest runway at Honolulu airport. He would have to land the plane at 195 miles per hour, compared to the normal speed of 170 miles per hour. The jet weighed 610,000 pounds, well above Boeing's recommended maximum stress load of 564,000 pounds. Nevertheless, Captain Cronin made one of the smoothest landings the rest of the crew could remember, amid the cheers of the passengers.

Airline experts called the landing miraculous. The Captain's judgment in overriding standard recommended emergency procedures is credited with saving the plane and passengers.

A few days after the harrowing experience, an interviewer asked Captain Cronin about his first thoughts following the loss of the cargo door. He said, "I said a prayer for my passengers momentarily and then got back to business."[1]

The passengers who survived that night of terror can say a prayer for Captain Cronin. They can thank God that he was a man of such high competence.

Captain Cronin had accumulated over three decades of flying experience prior to the fateful night of February 24. During those years he had safely piloted hundreds of thousands of passengers to their destinations. It was his work.

Every so often we hear of stories like that of Captain Cronin, about how people who are just doing their jobs save the lives of others. A school crossing guard snatches a child from in front of a runaway truck. A morning newspaper boy comes across a home on fire and saves a family. A store clerk administers CPR after a customer drops to the floor with a heart attack. While the public sees these people as heroes, their frequent response to all the attention is, "I was just doing my job."

Much of this book has to do with ministry in the workplace. By this I mean not only a place of employment, but workplace in the broadest meaning of the term. We all work. We may not all be paid for what we do, but we all work. Surely a parent staying in the home to raise children has work to do. Surely a student preparing for the future has work to do. Even those in the twilight years of life work as they provide support to friends and family.

THE BIBLE AND WORK

The topic of work appears very early in the Bible. God's very first command to human beings was, "Be fruitful and multiply, and fill the earth and subdue it; and have dominion over the fish of the sea and over the birds of the air, and over every living thing that moves upon the earth" (Genesis 1:28 RSV).

Humankind certainly has multiplied and, in many respects, has subdued the earth. But "subdue" means to bring under control, not to destroy. As humankind grows in numbers and in technological sophistication, the danger increases that instead of controlling the earth we will rape it, deplete its resources, and pollute it to the point where it can no longer sustain life.

Likewise, in the creation story dealing with Adam and Eve, the Garden of Eden is first created so that Adam could be placed in it "to cultivate and guard it" (Genesis 2:15 TEV). But Adam and Eve disobey God, and Adam is punished: "You will have to work hard all your life to make it produce enough food for you" (Genesis 3:17 TEV). The Bible thus gives us two themes regarding work: First, as partners with God, we control and develop God's creation through our work. And second, because of our rebellious nature, we are destined to work hard and sweat in order to exist. The concept that work is both a blessing and a bane is woven throughout the Bible and into the experience of God's people.

Some people experience their work as a blessing, while others—even in exactly the same type of job—say work is a "pain in the neck." There is great wisdom in the Genesis stories. Those who submit themselves to God's rule in their lives find joy and meaning in their work; those who totally rebel against God's authority see work only as a necessary evil to achieve certain personal goals or desires.

Most of us, however, are in that middle ground where a struggle rages between submitting to God or following our own selfish instincts. Accordingly, we may at times find meaning in our work and at other times find only drudgery. It seems clear, however, that God's will is for humankind to be in such a close relationship with God that we continue the process of creation in a responsible and caring way.

That's all very nice biblical theory, but it's hard to apply in a busy workday when the boss wants greater production, when the kids are constantly fighting with each other, when a traffic jam on the expressway makes you late for an important appointment, or when you're asked to do extra work because one of your coworkers did not show up on the job. How on earth do we see ourselves as cocreators with God in all this mess?

It is not easy; and I must confess that, for most of my life, I never even considered my work to be in partnership with God. I cannot recall an instance when I felt God's presence in selling steel. I felt God's presence in church on Sunday, or in the beauty of nature, or at points of pain or loss among friends and family. But God's presence in a customer's office? Never.

Yet, just because we do not see something, it does not mean that it is not there. Although I am a Lutheran, the Roman Catholic laity are helping me to grow in my perception of God's presence in my daily life, even in the hectic moments of a workday.

A SPIRITUALITY OF WORK

In his encyclical *On Human Work,* Pope John Paul II coined the term "spirituality of work." For most of my life the term "spirituality" referred to such religious acts as saying prayers, reading the Bible, meditating, and going to church. When one felt inclined to deepen one's spiritual life, it usually meant getting away from the world—to a retreat or monastic setting—and to spend time in study, meditation, and prayer. But here John Paul II talks of "a spirituality of work which will help all people to come closer, through work, to God, the Creator and Redeemer."[2]

The US Roman Catholic laity, at the National Center for the Laity in Chicago, are developing the concept of a spirituality of work in ways that make sense to people. Gregory Pierce, president of the Center, writes, "A spirituality of work necessitates orienting ourselves toward the divine through our daily activity of improving and sustaining the world."[3] Pierce and his associate, William Droel, have been working on some excellent small books intended to help people develop a spirituality of work in various occupational settings. The authors emphasize that they are not equating work with a paid job, but rather are using the understanding of Vatican II that "work refers to any human activity that cooperates with God's ongoing creation."[4]

Droel and Pierce point out that the language of the church—words like salvation, creation, redemption, sanctification, and others—must be given meaning in the language of the workplace. Otherwise, laypeople cannot connect their Sunday worship with their weekday work:

> Until now, laypeople have not had much help in seeing any part of their work as a spiritual experience. If laypeople cannot find any spiritual meaning in their work, they are condemned to living a certain dual life; not connecting what they do on Sunday morning with what they do the rest of the week. They need to discover that the very actions of daily life are spiritual, and enable laypeople to touch God *in* the world, not away from it. Such a spirituality will say to the layperson worried about lack of time for prayer: "Your work is your prayer."[5]

This is not a new theology by any means. Martin Luther spoke of the Bible being in the hands and heart of a worker. "Only look at your tools," Luther wrote, "your needle, your thimble, your beer barrel, your articles of trade, your scales, your measures, and you will find this saying written on them. . . . My dear, use me toward your neighbor as you would want him to act toward you with that which is his."[6]

Although the Reformation did articulate a theology of the spirituality of work, the church was never able to realize in practice what was being said in theory. I believe the people at the National Center for the Laity are helping us to put the theory into practice.

THE MINISTRY OF COMPETENCY

Through our work we can touch God in a variety of ways, and this theme will be developed in succeeding chapters. But if the call of the Christian is to participate in God's ongoing creative process, the bedrock foundation of our ministry has to be competency. We must use our talents in as competent a manner as possible.

When United Airlines Flight 811 got into trouble, the greatest gift Captain Cronin had for his passengers was his experience as a pilot and his good judgment. In those moments of peril, it mattered not to the passengers how Captain Cronin related to his coworkers or how he communicated his faith to others or what his lifestyle was like. The critical issue was this: Was he competent enough as a pilot to bring that badly damaged plane in safely?

Competence is our basic level of ministry. Tradition has it that St. Augustine was criticized by his Christian friends because he bought his sandals from a non-Christian craftsman when there was a Christian sandal maker in the same town. He defended his actions by explaining that he did too much walking to buy inferior sandals.

Competency is a basic value. It is not a means to some other end, such as wealth or position, although such results may occur. Lynn Wilson, the highly successful president of her own commercial design firm, comments on the exceptional growth of her $250 million dollar business: "My progress really has been generated not by a quest for being bigger, but really a quest for being better. My progress has really been a demand that I made of myself to always do something that challenged me and made me grow as a creative spirit, not as a financial magnate."[7]

Author Dorothy L. Sayers criticized the church for not helping people see the importance of competency. She wrote, "The church's approach to an intelligent carpenter is usually confined to exhorting him not to be drunk and disorderly in his leisure hours and to come to church on Sundays. What the church should be telling him is this: that the very first demand that his religion makes upon him is that he should make good tables."[8]

The more developed our world becomes, the more crucial becomes the issue of competency. In earlier societies people had to be self-sufficient. Families generally provided for their own food, clothing, and shelter. Incompetency usually had a direct and immediate effect on the one who was incompetent.

As civilization developed, however, people began to depend on the work of others for certain goods and services. Luther addressed his words about tools to such craftsmen as tailors, shoemakers, and carpenters. Not only did these trades require special skills, but the quality of work extended to larger numbers of people—possibly an entire town or region.

Today, however, we have become a global community, a community so interconnected that events in one part of our world affects the lives of people in many other nations. The emissions from coal-fueled electric generating plants in Ohio kill trees and fish in eastern Canada. A nuclear power plant accident in the Soviet Union affects dairy farmers in Scandinavia. A citrus freeze in Florida sends welcome financial relief to citrus growers in Mexico. The slightest change in a US government economic indicator can send the stock markets soaring or tumbling in Tokyo, Sydney, Hong Kong, Frankfurt, and London. The pain of an Olympic athlete being injured in an accident is instantaneously shared by millions and millions of television viewers in every corner of the world.

The world has invaded our homes: a shirt from China, shoes from Taiwan, a hat from Italy, a jacket from Scotland, a bottle of wine from Bulgaria, a clock radio from Korea, a coffee cup from England, a flashlight from Hong Kong, an auto from Japan, beer from Australia, a compact disc from West Germany, a book from Singapore. On and on it goes.

Perhaps nowhere has this almost instant globalization of society been more keenly felt than in the United States. For the greater part of the twentieth century, this country has been the dominant economic, political, and military force in the world. US business and industry was the envy of all other nations. Our standard of living was second to none and far outshone that of nonindustrial countries. Backed by a powerful military presence, American foreign policy, however irrational it may have seemed, dominated world affairs. The United States was the epitome of a society that was energetic, prosperous, self-assured, and independent.

LOSS OF COMPETENCY

But things have changed.

The American steel industry, which once produced 45 percent of the world's steel, has become a shadow of its former self. In only thirty years, from the early 1950s to the 1980s, foreign imports of raw steel increased from 2 percent of the total market to over 20 percent. Add to this the steel market lost due to the importation of such steel-consuming products as automobiles and heavy machinery, and the loss of market is staggering.

Our automobile industry has suffered similar losses. In 1960 US automakers produced more than 75 percent of the world's autos. By 1988 that share had plummeted to less than 25 percent.

For most of the twentieth century, the United States had a trade surplus; but since 1970 it has experienced a growing trade debt that reached $171 billion in 1987. From 1950 to 1988 this country lost 30 percent of its total world exports.[9]

Part of that export loss came in the form of agricultural products. It was not only industry that suffered. The so-called Green Revolution in the Third World had an indirect affect on US farmers, with the result that what was a $27 billion export surplus in 1981 became a $7 billion surplus by 1987.[10]

The loss of America's industrial dominance resulted in a wrenching restructuring of the industrial work force. Many laid-off steelworkers, autoworkers, and heavy equipment workers were forced to find work at lower pay rates with small new businesses or in the service industry. Of the 13 million Americans who lost their jobs between January 1981 and January 1986, one-third have left the work force and over half of those who did find new jobs earn less than they did before.[11] As the real income of the average male worker fell, a greater number of married women with children entered the work force. In spite of this, the gross real weekly earnings of American families has been declining since 1972. Measured on the long scale of history, this sharp reversal of America's economic dominance in the world could be classified as an almost instantaneous collapse of a powerful giant.

To many Americans this economic reversal may demonstrate a failure of the greatest magnitude. Yet, from the world's perspective, it is a story of success. To a great extent the success of other industrial nations has its seeds in this country, when, following the end of World War II, the massive Marshall Plan was launched to rebuild the shattered remains of our defeated enemies. This effort, unmatched in human history, was built on the conviction that long-term global peace can exist only if all nations are economically prosperous. Today we see the results of that vision.

No one today regrets that we launched the Marshall Plan in 1945. What is regretted and criticized is the fact that America's competitiveness has been blunted. As the 1988 *Cuomo Commission Report* on trade and competitiveness pointed out, blame for America's loss of position can be shared by many.[12] Because our nation has never had a true industrial and trade policy, our industries were easy marks for foreign producers who, in many instances, had the benefit of governmental subsidies of one sort or another. American management's obsession with short-term profits at the expense of long-term viability kept much of our industry from modernizing in plant, equipment, and technology. The labor-management relationship became poisoned by a hierarchal management philosophy that ignored the basic needs of workers, with the result that disaffected workers lost interest in quality and productivity. Union demands reflected this disenchantment with the job. Labor and management were adversaries.

Along with and perhaps related to the reversal of America's dominant economic position came other disturbing developments within our society. Among the twenty largest industrial nations, for example, the United States is in last place in infant mortality rate. A baby born in Spain has a better chance of reaching age one than does one born in the United States. Similarly in the world community, we rank forty-ninth in literacy and eighth in longevity. Illiteracy among minority students stood at 40 percent in 1988.[13]

In standardized tests between 1983 and 1986, American high school seniors came in last in biology among students from thirteen countries, including Hungary and Singapore. They were eleventh in chemistry and ninth in physics.[14]

What has happened to the United States in the past forty years? Both in real terms and relative to most other nations, we have become less competent. We have slipped as an industrial nation. Our educational system is distressingly poor. Our health system increasingly benefits only those with money. Our family units are crumbling. Our prisons are overflowing.

These "macro" issues may seem overwhelming and unrelated

from the "micro" issues of our personal lives. Yet these problems do connect with each other and with each of us. We can bring competency into the micro issues of our own lives, but how can we possibly affect the macro issues of a slipping national competency?

The *Cuomo Commission Report* makes an interesting observation about the interplay between macroeconomic factors and microeconomic factors:

> Economists draw a distinction between microeconomics, the study of individual firms and small-scale phenomena, and macroeconomics, the study of national and international factors. We found that competitiveness is in many respects a microeconomic issue: how effectively does this factory produce this product; why are goods made here of better quality than goods made there?[15]

Our world is infinitely more interrelated than it was twenty years ago. It is infinitely more complex than it was a hundred years ago. And yet the macro issues that face us are directly related to a host of micro issues. It is in dealing with the smaller, personal issues of our lives that we can collectively affect the larger world issues.

I recall the time when a product that bore the stamp "Made in Japan" was certain to be of inferior quality. Everyone knew that. Today Japanese products carry the reputation of quality. What happened?

Knowing they had to produce quality products in order to compete in the world market, Japanese businesspeople set about to create the environment, in countless factories, that would turn things around. They concentrated on a work ethic, on innovative worker-manager relationships, on state-of-the-art production equipment, and on a common commitment to succeed in their goal. These were all micro issues for each individual manufacturing plant. But they succeeded; and that success contributed to one of the most outstanding macroeconomic feats of modern times: the emergence of Japan as a major industrial nation.

For us, too, there can be no large-scale changes in our nation until we have many small-scale changes. We must make changes in our families, our schools, our health systems, our industries, our governmental agencies, and our basic sense of values. It is Christians, who constitute the largest religious group in our nation, who must largely bear the responsibility for the deterioration of our institutions; it is Christians who must lead the way in turning things around.

In short, while a spirituality of work begins as a very personal thing for each of us, its implications for a nation can be monumental. But where should we begin?

We begin with ourselves. We need to begin to search for God in our places of work. God is already there, make no mistake about it; we simply have not trained ourselves to see our Creator.

I have been working on this spirituality of work for several years, and it has not been easy for me. During my morning prayer time, I consider my agenda for the day and pray that I will be open to God's action in these events. I must confess that when things get rolling during the day, I usually forget to ask myself, "Where is God in all this activity?" Not until later do I reflect on whether I was aware of God's presence in the events of my day. Most of the time the answer is no.

But sometimes I do remember to search for God's presence, with mixed results. I am most alert to God's presence when someone asks for my opinion on a personal problem. I inwardly take a deep breath and try my best to share whatever experience I may have that might help the other person. Those moments can be awesome because, if I let it happen, God's message may be breaking through to someone in need.

At other times I searched for God's presence and did not find it—at least, not at that moment. Sometime ago, for example, one of my clients was in the process of buying a part of another company from an unscrupulous owner. The seller had purchased this company about two years earlier. He milked the company for his own personal welfare, and when it became too weak to survive, he began to liquidate it in pieces. He had a long record of not living up to his word. Scores of creditors were trying to collect money he owed them. More than once his reserves were so low that the paychecks to the employees bounced. The morale among the employees was terrible. Yet they hung on because they needed to add time toward their pensions—if there would ever be a pension fund left.

I helped my client determine the worth of the part of the company that we wanted to buy. Soon things were in order for the final negotiations, and we met on the thirtieth floor of a Boston law firm on a bright, sunny day in spring. Sitting across the long conference table from us were two officers of the seller's company and two of their lawyers. On our side of the table were my client, one of his vice presidents, two lawyers, and I.

The negotiations were difficult. The record of dishonesty of the seller's company meant that every statement they made had to be clarified in detail and verified, if possible. When you distrust others, they quickly begin to distrust you. We were adversaries trying to make a deal, but always suspecting the other party was tricking us. Time after time, one party or the other would adjourn to another room for a caucus and return with new strategies.

After about six hours of this high-tension negotiating process, I left my seat and walked over to the picture window overlooking Boston harbor. It was a beautiful day outside. The sunlight sparkled on the water, and across the way I could see jetliners gliding into Logan Airport. I said to myself, "God, where are you? I see you out there, but I surely don't see you in this room." I listened, but got no answer. I returned to my seat, and we finally concluded negotiations about three hours later.

The following morning found me in another conference room, that of my client. Across the table were three employees of the company we had just purchased. They had come in to learn of the details of the purchase. On my side of the table were the same people—minus the lawyers—who had been negotiating for my client the previous day. The new employees were excited to learn that my client, who had a very good reputation, was their new owner. We heard story after story of how terrible it had been working for the old owner. It was really sad to hear how badly people could be treated by an employer.

Finally, after the terrible stories had been told, the vice president sitting next to me said, "Well, isn't it appropriate that this is Holy Week? It looks like you chaps are experiencing a resurrection!"

I was a bit shocked to hear this simile, but one of the new employees quickly came back with, "Yeah, you know, you're right. I feel like the stone has just been rolled away!"

There it was, and I had been too blind to see it. What had been going on in those nine hours of hard negotiations was the rescue of jobs and a new chance for some mighty fine people. We had secured their jobs and their pensions and given them a new future under a much better owner. The part of it all that still surprises me is that it was two men who never before had used religious images in the workplace who saw the connection I was searching for.

From this experience I learned two great lessons. First, it is harder to see God's presence in the ongoing events of life than it is to see God's presence after they have happened. And second, that look as we might, God sometimes is revealed to us through the eyes of others.

PERCEIVING GOD'S PRESENCE

However the answer comes, I remain convinced that we need to keep asking the question, "Where is God in this situation?" For when we do this, we are bringing spirituality into our workplace, and we more readily see the need for competency.

It is easier to sense God's presence in the workplace when people are obviously being helped. The field of health care is the most likely place to discern the presence of God. Jesus' ministry is filled with accounts of restoring people to health. Christians in health and human services occupations are usually able to talk openly and with ease about sensing God's presence in their places of work.

The field of education is a close second to health care since it, too, is dedicated to serving people. While many teachers today are suffering from burnout, due to the difficult conditions under which they must work, they generally do acknowledge that there is a real Christian ministry in teaching. Jesus met the needs of people through his teaching ministry. So, while it may be difficult to see God's presence when one is trying to maintain discipline in a disruptive classroom, most teachers I have talked to concede that, upon reflection, they can discern that presence.

Mothers, as primary caregivers and teachers, whether or not they work outside the home, are in an excellent position to discern God's presence in their places of work. Unfortunately, our society has too greatly undervalued parenthood in favor of work outside the home. The Christian community needs to correct this wrong emphasis, for the ministry of parenthood is very close to the heart of God.

Those who care for people through our legal and justice systems can usually see their lives in ministry. Police and firefighters can do so. Captain Cronin, the pilot of Flight 811, can do so. Clearly, Christian ministry in the workplace is most readily seen in those occupations in which care is directly provided to people. The more removed our work is from the direct service to people, the more difficult it is to see our Christian ministry, and therefore, the more difficult, to develop a sense of God's presence in our work.

We can see this with tradespeople and craftspeople. The shoe repair person who sees his or her customers personally is in a better position to see a ministry of competency than one who works in a shoe factory hundreds of miles away from faceless customers. The plumber who repairs a problem in your home is in a better position to see competency in work as ministry than the plumber installing systems in unoccupied houses in a new development.

The more removed work is from direct service to people, the more we have to stretch to try to convince people that there is ministry in their work. For example, a farmer provides food for people. That's ministry. What about the factory worker who assembles farm equipment? Well, yes, that's serving God's people, because if it weren't for farm equipment, less food would be grown and fewer people would benefit. What about the steelworker in the forge shop who stamps out a slug of steel that will later be machined down into an axle for a piece of farm equipment? Well, yes, we can say that since the steel axle is needed for the farm equipment so that food can be grown, the steelworker also is in ministry.

That's fine in theory, but don't ever ask a steelworker in a drop forge shop if he sees ministry in his work. He will point out that day after day he stands at the same drop forge in a hot and dirty shop, holding heavy slugs of hot steel and activating a drop hammer with his foot so that he can shape the steel into some form with no idea of what its end use will be. He will tell you that it is so noisy in that shop that all the workers use ear protectors and consequently he can't even talk to anybody. Why does he work there? "The pay is good, and I can provide a living for my family," he will invariably reply.

The truth is that in some jobs workers are hard pressed to see how they minister to society. In this area we need the creativeness of competent managers. We have learned from the Japanese that by restructuring jobs in such a way that small groups of workers are responsible for the output of their unit, both quality and productivity increase. More of that approach to management is creeping into American industry today. It is another example of a micro change that has the potential of contributing to the macro change in America's competitiveness. The side benefit of all this is that the chances are greater that all workers will be able to see how their work contributes to God's creation.

I learned the importance of competency as a young steel salesman in Detroit. My job was to sell steel products for the construction of buildings and bridges. We, Bethlehem Steel, had a small steel fabricating plant in Detroit that produced fabricated reinforcing bars for reinforced concrete structures. I immediately observed that every time my car pulled into the parking lot of the shop, the foreman and one or two other workers would come out to talk to me. They wanted to know how I was doing. If I had a roll of blueprints under my arm, it was usually a sign that I had just landed a new contract for them to work on. It was obvious to me that they were depending on me to get contracts so that they could work and so that their families could be fed, clothed, and housed. To the extent that I was a competent salesman, I ministered to them.

Later, when I was manager of sales, and had to deal with a salesperson who was coasting—possibly because he was nearing retirement—I stressed the point that there was much more at stake than this one job. We had to consider the unseen thousands of workers in our steel plants. They were counting on us to do a competent sales job so that they, in turn, would have employment.

I believe we serve God's creation not only by committing ourselves to competency, but also by encouraging and motivating others. One way of doing this is to recognize and reward competence when we see it.

When the teenager down the street does a good job of mowing my lawn or shoveling the snow, do I compliment him? Is the woman who comes in weekly to help with household chores complimented on her work if it is done well? If the person at the checkout counter in the supermarket is friendly, helpful, and accurate, do we communicate our appreciation?

When I am interviewed for a newspaper or magazine story, I always try to be helpful to the reporter. At the close of the interview, I invariably thank the interviewer, in advance, for his or her ministry to me. That always evokes another question: What did I mean by that? To which I reply that a story about me is now in their hands and I am counting on them to quote me accurately. To the extent they do, I point out, they are ministering both to me and to their readers. I am counting on them to be competent. That is part of their ministry.

In most cases they have an intellectual understanding of the point I am making. But on one occasion I happened to say this to a reporter who had left her church out of disillusionment. She was absolutely fascinated by this concept of ministry, and we talked for some time about it. Several years later we met by chance, and she reminded me of our conversation. "I want you to know," she said, "that when you told me that I had a ministry as a reporter, something clicked inside of me. I knew it was true, and I remind myself of it every time I do a story. I've gone back to my church. Things aren't much better there than when I left, but it doesn't matter anymore. I know I am witnessing to my faith by the quality of my work."

Wow!

NOT ALL WORK IS MINISTRY

Although the scope of ministry in the workplace is very broad, not every occupation can be claimed as Christian ministry. If an occupation is clearly destructive or harmful to others, it cannot be a field for Christian ministry. A drug pusher, or one who exploits children to produce pornographic videos, cannot lay claim to Christian ministry, even though they might point to some charitable deeds they do with the income from such work. Fortunately, societies protect against harm to people through laws. If a type of work is illegal, it is clearly ruled out as Christian ministry.

But in some gray areas Christians differ on the propriety of work. While most Christians think that serving in the military is a necessary and therefore acceptable occupation, there appears to be less support for work in a plant producing nuclear weapons. Even though both a standing army and the availability of nuclear weapons can be claimed to be effective deterrents against war, some people will support an occupation in the former but reject it in the latter. Similarly, some church members will reject jobs in the tobacco and beverage alcohol industries. There are sharp divisions over jobs related to providing abortions. I have spoken with some Christians who see no socially redeeming purpose in working on

"Wall Street," as they characterize the securities trading occupations. Others oppose work in the advertising field, or for transnational corporations, or for companies doing business in South Africa.

While we may have differences of opinion of whether certain jobs truly represent arenas for Christian ministry, we need to be cautious about becoming too restrictive in our list, because all of creation is the object of God's love and concerns, not just those parts that agree with our own personal values or political beliefs. Furthermore, while I see no redeeming value in producing cigarettes, until such time as our society outlaws them or voluntarily gives them up, some people will be hired to work in cigarette factories. Is it better that there be no Christians in those factories, or is some form of Christian presence desirable?

DEMAND COMPETENCY

Equally important, just as we can expect and reward competence on a one-to-one basis, we need to demand it from the structures of our society. As citizens and voters, we must demand quality education for all children in this country. We must find a way to break the deadly cycle of poverty, illiteracy, and crime. It is an absolute scandal that the United States of America should rank forty-ninth among the nations of the world in literacy.

We should demand that there be safe places of shelter for all who are without homes, that there be health services available for all in need, and that no human being should go without food. These are basic needs for all of God's creatures. Whether these needs are best met through the private sector, the public sector, or the volunteer sector can be debated and tested, but there can be no debate that the institutions of this nation must be competent enough to meet these needs. How we deal with the competency of our structures of society will be dealt with in the chapters on a ministry of change.

Work is a part of God's plan for humankind. We are called on to continue God's creative process through the work that we do. Our greatest witness to our faith in our places of work is our degree of competency. Unless we are competent, our witness as Christians is not seriously received by this world.

CHAPTER 3

Competency and Competition

As manager of sales at Bethlehem Steel, I pressed our salespeople to be very competent so that we would get orders and the people in our mills and factories could continue to work. It was an especially heavy responsibility during periods of recession or a falling off in the demand for steel.

The steel industry is very dependent on steel-consuming industries for its livelihood. If American automobiles, appliances, machinery, steel cans, and construction products are selling well, the steel industry does well. It is very difficult for the steel industry to create demand for its product because it is almost totally dependent on these other industries. In any given year, the size of the steel market is determined by others. Each steel company competes for a share of that fixed market.

And so, as I urged our salespeople to do better in those lean years, I often wondered if my urgings for greater competency were helping to turn out the lights of our competitors' plants in Youngstown, Gary, Pittsburgh, or Birmingham. I knew I had a clear responsibility to the employees of our company, but I pondered whether I also had a responsibility to the workers in our competitors' plants.

As we apply principles of the Christian faith to our daily lives, we frequently encounter the "yes, but" questions that nag at us. As participants in God's ongoing work of creation, we are called on to use our talents to the glory of God. That's fine for an artist or composer or craftsman. But many of us work in a competitive environment. What if we are so competent that our competitor is hurt? Does it matter at all?

Some might say that when organizations compete against each other, be it in sports or business, a type of Darwinism applies. Society is best served if the strong organizations survive and the weak ones die to make place for new competitors. That was the way I resolved my thinking with respect to the other steel companies with which we competed. Yes, the employees of an incompetent steel company might be hurt by our high competency, but in our success we might well be offering new jobs to others as we grew. Besides, the public benefits from aggressive business competition in the marketplace. Sounds reasonable, doesn't it? But what if competition involves a specific person we know?

BERT

It was about 9:00 P.M. when the phone rang.

"Hi, Bill, it's Bert."

"Bert?" I asked, not recognizing the voice.

"Yeah, you know, Bert Thompson."

I was somewhat astonished. Albert Thompson was one of my competitors. He was in his late sixties and was the owner of a small construction materials company, which he had developed from scratch. A number of the products I sold were in direct competition with some of his.

"Listen, Bill, I'm calling to see if we can arrange to meet sometime soon. I need to talk to you about this market."

"Bert, you know I can't meet with you. It's against the law."

"Oh, this isn't going to be anything big. I just want you to understand how your aggressive selling is hurting my business."

I wasn't surprised to hear that. As a young, energetic salesman, I was getting around the state a lot more than he was. I was able to pick up some orders from some of his longtime customers. He just didn't have the energy to keep up with my pace.

"No, Bert, I absolutely cannot meet with you at any time or place."

"Well, then, you listen to this," he persisted. "You are ruining a business I spent my whole life developing. If you keep this up, I'll go bankrupt."

"Bert, I'm not responsible for your problems," I pleaded.

"Yes, you are, young man," he shouted. "And let me tell you this: If you drive me into bankruptcy, I'll kill myself and you will be to blame!"

I put down the receiver. Am I my brother's keeper? I asked myself. I was frightened. Might he really do it?

OUR COMPETITIVE SOCIETY

We live in a highly competitive society. Competition has so completely permeated our lives that we scarcely think about it. Television, the newest member of the American family, pours out a steady stream of messages in which products and services compete for our money. Through television, we are able to have a continuous exposure to competitive sports—football, baseball, basketball, the Olympics, boxing, wrestling, all types of racing, golf, tennis, bowling, and on it goes. The sheer volume of competitive sports that enters our homes through television far exceeds the exposure people had to it fifty years ago. Add to it all a steady stream of TV game shows, and the effect is stunning.

Our children taste competition in early school years as they enter sports and learn that the world rewards those who do well with lots of money. They learn quickly that one's material possessions are the measure of success in a competitive society.

There is competition aplenty in business, but, it is just as pervasive in the performing arts and in journalism as people compete for Oscars, Emmys, Obies, and Pulitzer prizes. Rural America competes for prizes at the county fair; suburban America competes for the best-kept lawn on the block.

Everything is ranked: the ten best major universities, the most livable cities, the best corporations, the finest symphony orchestras, the best zoo, the tallest building, the longest bridge.

Well, what's wrong with all this competition? What do you expect if we all do our best to be competent? Doesn't the commitment to competency in itself create competition?

There are those who say that competition is destructive. Competition creates winners and losers. On the other hand, they say, cooperation creates only winners.

THE BIBLE AND COMPETITION

The Bible presents contrasting messages on the issue. The Old Testament provides numerous accounts of how God assists his people to win over their adversaries. Moses frustrated the Egyptians, Gideon defeated the Midianites, Joshua took Jericho. But, in the New Testament, Jesus says, "If any one would be first, he must be last of all and servant of all" (Mark 9:35 RSV). He urged people to humble themselves and to take the lowest seat at a banquet (Luke 14:7–11). He told a story in which those who worked for only the last hour of the day were paid the first and received as much for their labor as those who worked all day (Matthew 20:1–16). Yet the apostle Paul, in his letters to the young churches, makes references to overcoming the forces of evil and of running a good race (Romans 12:21; 1 Corinthians 9:24–27).

I find it difficult to make a case one way or the other on competition, based on specific Bible references. Two themes that apply to competition do run through the Bible, however, and their intersection in our daily lives do present us with problems.

The first theme is that of being called by God to continue the creative process in partnership with God. This theme leads us in the direction of competency, which was discussed in the previous chapter. The history of the Christian church is sprinkled with the accounts of people who, in dedicating their life's work in God's service, were extraordinarily competent in their work—composers, writers, artists, educators, political leaders, scientists, physicians. When we dedicate our life's work to the glory of God, we strive to do our absolute best.

The other theme first appears also in Genesis. In response to God's question to Cain about the whereabouts of his brother, Abel, we encounter those plaintive words that have echoed through the ages: "Am I my brother's keeper?" (Genesis 4:9 RSV). The Old Testament is filled with admonitions to care for those who are poor and powerless. The book of Leviticus is very specific in how such care should be expressed:

> If a fellow Israelite living near you becomes poor and cannot support himself, you must provide for him as you would for a hired man, so that he can continue to live near you. Do not

charge him any interest, but obey God and let your fellow
Israelite live near you. Do not make him pay interest on the
money you lend him and do not make a profit on the food
you sell him. (Leviticus 25:35–37 TEV)

Concern for the poor, the widow, the orphan, the disabled, the
elderly, the visitor abound in the Psalms and the prophetical books,
and this theme continues in the New Testament. Jesus sharply condemned the hypocrisy of the teachers and Pharisees who exalted
themselves and neglected the important teachings of the Law,
"such as justice, and mercy and honesty" (Matthew 23:23 TEV). He
frequently turned conventional wisdom around: "The last shall be
first and the first last" (Matthew 20:16 RSV).

In his parable of the Good Samaritan, it was the highly competent and busy priest and Levite who "passed by on the other
side" when they saw the wounded traveler. But a lowly and less
esteemed Samaritan became the hero of the story (Luke 10:30–37).

The New Testament letters make frequent mention of caring for
the less fortunate. There are warnings also for those who, by competency or birth, are wealthy and who run the risk of loving money
instead of God (1 Timothy 6:7–10).

Christians are called to be good stewards of the gifts God has
given them. We are to be both competent and compassionate.
Sometimes those qualities can be in tension with each other. What
do we do then?

THE CONSEQUENCES OF COMPETITION

For many people the call to competency and the call to care for
those less fortunate do not come into conflict. But occasionally, in
a competitive society, they do. As Christians, we have to weigh the
probable consequences of our actions and decide whether we
should ease up on the drive for competency in order to care for one
less fortunate, or whether we should do our best regardless of the
possible results. The problem is, we never know for sure how our
decisions to act or not to act will turn out. So we study the issue,
seek God's guidance through prayer, and then boldly do what we
think is right.

In the instance cited at the beginning of this chapter, I concluded that my responsibility to our own workers in a recessionary period was at least as great as my responsibility to the workers for competing steel companies. Furthermore, our government has laws designed to prevent unfair competitive practices that would give large companies an advantage over smaller competitors. The laws don't always work as envisioned, but they do provide some measure of fairness in the marketplace. Finally, if we accept the principle that the survival of the weakest economic competitors is not the best for a society, then, as a Christian manager of sales, I can urge our sales force to press hard for orders—even if our competitors have to cut back on their operations.

The situation with Bert was more troubling. Here it was my personal efforts of hard work and competency that were allegedly driving his business into the ground.

The antitrust laws made one option clear: I could not meet with him to discuss prices or customers or share of market or geographic territories. But I did have the option to decide to be less aggressive where his longstanding customers were involved. There would be no agreement between us, and I would never acknowledge the fact to him. I would just ease up on competing with him.

Were there other options? Did I even have a responsibility to him? Was I Bert's "keeper"? I took the problem first to my pastor. The trouble was that he was unaware of the antitrust laws and kept suggesting various ways of arriving at an "arrangement" with Bert. One thing came in clear from my pastor, however: He was convinced I had some responsibility toward Bert.

I next went to my boss, Don Bradley, and got what turned out to be solid advice. He was pleased that I had immediately rejected the request to meet, based on my knowledge of the antitrust laws. He correctly judged that I was considering easing off in my competition with Bert, but he instructed me not to do so.

"Look, Bill," he said in a fatherly manner, "you are a nice young man, but you are naive. Bert is trying to do a number on you. He is not going to kill himself because of your success. He's trying to scare you. If his business is as bad as he suggests, he could sell it to his younger salesman and retire now." Then he concluded with a more direct statement. "If I discover that you have met with him over this matter, you will be fired!" That got my attention. "Furthermore, this company hired you to give us your best effort. If you hold back, you are, in a sense, stealing from your employer." I hadn't thought of that.

Don's assessment and advice were flawless, as it turned out. I kept doing my best. In about a year Bert sold the company to his younger salesman and retired in comfort.

I learned an important lesson through this experience. Pastors are not always the appropriate people to consult when a Christian is trying to relate faith to daily life. Pastors are not competent to provide counsel in all types of problems, nor should they be expected to do so. So where do we go with the more technical problems? We go to the church, the community of believers.

In the wide Christian community there are thousands of people who long to apply the principles of their faith to the problems of daily life. Each of us, as a practitioner of some type of work, should develop a small support group of Christians who have competency in our field of endeavor. We should meet with them regularly to share experiences and solicit advice when we need it. My boss, Don Bradley, was my person of competence. He was also a strong churchgoing person, although the topic of religious teachings never came up directly in our conversation. But it would have been more helpful if there had been a group of six or eight Christian business-people with whom I had an ongoing relationship. In such an environment there undoubtedly would have been open conversation about faith and life and, quite likely, prayer for guidance. Much more will be said about support groups throughout this book.

One final comment on the story of Bert. I sometimes use the story in my ministry in the workplace conferences as a real-life case study of the dilemmas Christians often face in the workplace. After going through an extensive discussion of the case with conference participants and then reporting on the outcome, I sometimes am asked the question, "But how would you have felt if Bert had actually committed suicide?" Frankly, I would have felt terrible. I think I could have rationalized it all intellectually, but in my gut I would have felt real pain.

It is not helpful for Christians to deal with the problems of a competitive society by declaring, "We should give up all competition and work at cooperation." That can be done in some small degree, but we are dealing with a massive and institutionalized cultural phenomenon that will not go away. It seems to be part of human nature. Rather, we need to recognize the reality of competition and deal with the situations that cause us problems.

In some sports we have developed ways to make competition fairer through various types of handicapping. Golf is an excellent example. The excellent golfer with a low handicap must concede a certain number of strokes to a hacker with a high handicap before they even begin to play. If the handicaps have been accurately computed, a round of golf between an expert and an average player will be very close in net score. Should there be a system of handicaps in business also?

Team sports, such as professional football, have a system of annual drafts of new players in which the worst teams from the previous season get the first picks of the available pool of new players. The process is intended to even out the talent throughout the league over a period of years. It does work to some extent.

I greatly admire those Little League coaches who insist that every player on the team will have an equal opportunity to bat and field the ball, no matter what the score. Winning is not everything.

The business system in the United States operates under certain laws designed to prevent one competitor from becoming so dominant in its industry that it has a monopoly. There have been times when the US government has intervened in the competitive marketplace to prevent a weak competitor from going out of business. The best-remembered examples are the so-called bailouts of Chrysler and Lockheed. Voluntary import quotas and duties protect many American businesses from the kind of unfair foreign competition that can cause massive unemployment in this country. And finally, there are federal, state, and local laws and regulations that control the behavior of business organizations with regard to employment practices, consumer protection, environmental concerns, occupational health and safety, and many other areas. It has been argued that the body of regulations, intended to make business competition in the United States fair and responsible, is now so massive that it is almost impossible for new competitors to enter certain industries. In other words, while some laws try to prevent monopolies, other laws tend to promote them. The claim that we have a totally free market system is not accurate.

The point is, however, that our society has decided to put certain controls on the competitive system of American business.

These controls are intended to make competition open and fair, and at the same time protect employees, customers, and society from possible abuses connected with unbridled competition.

OUR JUDICIAL SYSTEM

In some areas of American society competition is so built into the system that little can be done to correct injustices. For example, we have built our whole judicial system to be a highly competitive adversarial process that can cause problems for the practitioners. We're not about to change the system, so we have to find ways to help those who struggle with the dilemmas. Let me be specific.

As manager of sales at Bethlehem Steel, I occasionally became involved in civil lawsuits growing out of contract disputes. It was interesting to observe how our adversarial judicial system focused our law department on one thing only: winning the case.

We made every effort to secure the best outside counsel to represent us, given the nature of the case and where it would be tried. Our law department kept book on those lawyers who were "winners" in the courtroom.

Contract disputes can be very complex, and seldom is there any totally right or wrong litigant. Usually, the disputes involve gray areas. Competent lawyers skillfully promote their client's strong points and aggressively attack their opponent's weak points. They seek expert witnesses who have high courtroom credibility. Everything focuses on winning the case.

If both sides are represented by equally competent lawyers, the adversarial process should theoretically yield a just resolution of the dispute. But not all lawyers are of equal competence. What happens if one side has a highly competent attorney and the other side does not? Is justice served?

I have been in courtrooms where there were obvious differences in the competency of opposing counsels. It's a great feeling when your side is winning. But when you lose a case in which you know you were right, simply because the other side had a more competent lawyer, the system seems to be grossly unfair.

In discussions with lawyer friends, I have found that lawyers, as Christians, do agonize over apparent injustices that slip through the system. Poor people cannot afford the most skillful lawyers. If, during the course of a trial, a highly skilled attorney discovers the opponent in court is represented by a very incompetent lawyer, should he or she still try to win? If an elderly person is suing a major corporation, the defense lawyer will do well to delay bringing the case to court in the hope that the plaintiff will die before the trial begins. Does the call to competency cause a lawyer to use such stall tactics, since they are not illegal?

Once a lawyer accepts a client's case, is he or she bound to the lawyer-client confidentiality rule? If the lawyer discovers some information that, if revealed, could correct a prior error of justice, can the lawyer-client confidentiality be breached?

Competent lawyers are called to win cases. Should they ever be concerned about the opposing side?

The matter of competency within a competitive environment is only one issue Christians have to face in the workplace. There are others. For example, how do we deal with the incompetency or indifference of our workplace associates? Moreover, since competency relates to how well we do our work, is there a danger that Christians will appear to be promoting a theology of works righteousness? By claiming that competency is the basic level of ministry in the workplace, do we place too much emphasis on what we do for God rather than what God can do through us? These are legitimate concerns and will be dealt with in subsequent chapters.

OCCUPATIONAL SUPPORT GROUPS

Given the kinds of dilemmas faced by Christians in the workplace, how do we determine the best way to witness to our faith in specific situations? Without doubt, the best resource is a Christian support group made up of competent practitioners working in the same or similar fields of work.

An optimum group consists of from six to twelve people who have made a commitment to each other to meet on a regular basis for the purpose of sharing their experiences and concerns as they try to live out their faith in their daily lives. The group pledges to maintain confidentiality of sensitive issues.

Sometimes such groups can be composed of people working within the same organization, but there is always the risk that someone will violate the confidentiality pact. It has been my experience that Christian support groups within a single organization tend to focus on Bible study and prayer, which is great; but the environment is not the best for discussing sensitive topics.

The most effective support groups for ministry in the workplace are those composed of people from somewhat similar work situations. But be careful of the mix. If people are too like-minded, the chances for developing new or creative options for solving a problem are diminished. Having only senior managers in a support group has the advantage of finding a commonality of experience sharing, but at the expense of learning how a problem is perceived by a lower-level employee or a customer. It is best to aim for a diversity of people who work in a similar field. So don't mix physicians with businesspeople, but do have one support group for people in health care and another for people in business.

The occupational support group can be ecumenical or wholly from one congregation. The ecumenical approach offers the possibility of a greater variety of biblical and theological perspectives, but also poses the potential for debating denominational differences instead of dealing with workplace issues. In my experience laypeople are far less concerned about differences between denominations than are the clergy. The chances for friction over these differences are very small.

The Monday Connection

The Monday Connection is an occupational support group composed entirely of people from my congregation. We meet the first Monday of each month for breakfast at the Superior Diner in Emmaus, Pennsylvania, at 7:00 A.M. We are always done by 8:00 A.M. and on our way to work. About twenty-five of us participate in the program, but our attendance is usually between fourteen and eighteen due to travel and job demands. About three-quarters of the group is male, one-quarter female. While most of the people are connected with some form of business, the range is large. Several men are senior executives with local divisions of major corporations. Some of the participants own small businesses. Some are in industrial settings; others are in service industries. Our congregation's director of lay ministries always attends, and our senior pastor usually does.

For each monthly session one of the members volunteers to do a real-life case study of a problem he or she is facing. Usually, the case study is job-related, but it is acceptable to introduce family or community problems.

We arrive promptly at 7:00 A.M. and order breakfast. One person offers prayer. The copies of the case study are distributed as we eat. By 7:20 A.M. we are prepared to discuss the problem. More often than not, someone in the group has experienced a similar problem and relates what happened. The presenter is asked questions for clarification and then the group begins to explore possible action options. We never tell someone what to do and we are never judgmental. We simply try to help the person examine as many options as possible.

The role of the pastor is one of listener and biblical/theological resource. At times the pastor may point to biblical or theological perspectives that may be relevant to our discussion. Naturally, if the pastor has had an experience similar to that of the case study, he or she is as free as any participant to tell of it.

Whenever possible, a member of the clergy or a competent Bible scholar should be part of any support group—because, frankly, most laypeople are biblical illiterates. If some of the members of the group are well versed in the Bible, the clergy presence is not needed. On the other hand, for a clergy person to be part of an occupational support does provide a valuable learning experience for the clergy person in how to support their laity for ministry in daily life. One caution, however: Do not expect, or even permit, the clergy person to be the all-knowing authority on all subjects. He or she is a resource person and equal partner in the support group. No clergy person, or any member of the group, should be allowed to dominate the discussions.

One aspect of our Monday Connection work is unique: We ask the presenter of the case study to pay close attention during the Sunday worship of the day before our breakfast for "connections." Do any elements of the worship service—such as the lessons, the sermon, the liturgy, the hymns, or the prayers—relate or connect to the case study? The presenter shares that information with the group. Sometimes there are clear connections; more often than not, however, the presenter cannot discern any. This fact has caused the pastor to consider ways in which the worship service can be more relevant to the concerns that people bring with them on Sunday morning.

Why is the occupational support group a necessary resource for ministry in the workplace? Because it provides a channel through which we can discern God's will in a given situation. When faced with dilemmas in our work, we call upon the resources of our faith. We pray. We consult the Scriptures. We take it to our brothers and sisters in the faith. What better human resource can we turn to than that of committed Christians of competence and compassion who are living out their faith in workplaces similar to ours? What more likely channel might God use in responding to our prayers for guidance?

Starting a Support Group

It is tragic that so few congregations see the need to affirm, equip, and support people in their ministries in daily life. But such is a fact of life. It is usually up to laypeople to develop their own Christian support systems.

The Monday Connection was a support group I started. I simply sent a letter of explanation to about fifty people in our congregation and asked them to indicate if they were interested. About twenty-five responded positively. My secretary mails this group monthly postcard reminders, with a phone follow-up from those we do not hear from. One visit to the Superior Diner was all it took to give us a private section in the restaurant the first Monday of each month. That's it. No big deal. Anyone can do the same.

If it is not possible to establish a support group, a mentor might be the next best choice. Various ecumenical organizations train people to serve as mentors for men and women in business, so that they can relate faith to daily life.[1] The mentor meets on a one-to-one basis with the young businessperson to discuss the dimensions of ministry in the workplace and to be a supportive resource.

The Servant Society, operating out of Santa Barbara, California, under the leadership of Howard Blake, has as its mission to provide support and resources to senior executives in business and government who, for reasons of high confidentiality, cannot share their decision making concerns with their peers.[2]

If we seek to be competent in our ministries in the workplace, we need to establish an ongoing relationship with other Christians who are similarly trying to be faithful witnesses in their places of work. The combination of prayer, Bible study, and participation in a Christian support group will provide the way for us to develop a greater spirituality in our places of work.

III
PRESENCE

CHAPTER 4

Being There for Somebody

"Judy, why do you put up with it?" I asked with exasperation. "Why do all these women dump their problems on you?"

We were living in Detroit and were in the early years of child raising. Our neighborhood was heavily populated with young families in circumstances similar to ours: husband at work all day, wife at home with young kids, only one car in the family, money tight.

The women frequently got together for coffee in the morning and to supervise the children in play. In the afternoons, if the weather was nice, they clustered on one of the lawns. They were a natural support group to each other. "I'd go batty if I didn't have other adults to talk to during the day," Judy used to say. "I need some intellectual stimulation. Little children don't give you that."

But something else was happening, and it usually happened around the kitchen table in our little house. Sally Merkle was an unhappy woman, and her husband, Al, was a major part of it. She was very open in telling Judy about all her marital problems. Mickie Gross was concerned that Doug wasn't making it in his job. They were seven hundred miles away from home, and what would happen to them if Doug lost his job? Joanne Gray, who came from a well-to-do family, wanted a life-style that her husband, Walter, was unable to deliver as a young draftsman working his way through college. She was irritated with his lack of drive.

For some reason it was around our kitchen table where all these family problems, fears, and frustrations were unloaded. I felt it was terribly unfair to Judy that all the women in the neighborhood came to her with their tales of woe. I frequently urged Judy to tell her friends to keep their problems to themselves. She didn't, and the pattern continued until we moved.

Looking back on those days, we now realize several things.

First, something about Judy allowed other women to share their concerns. Undoubtedly, a large part of it was Judy's nonjudgmental nature. She was, and still is, a good listener. She seldom places blame or lays guilt on others. She is supportive of others in a low-key way. It is one of her gifts.

Second, in those days, neither of us realized that the exercising of Judy's gift was her ministry. In fact, in the early 1950s, neither of us saw Christian ministry as existing outside the structure of our congregation. Today we realize that she had quite a ministry going on Pembroke Road in Detroit. She was a competent mother and homemaker. We have a beautiful family, with excellent values, as living proof of that. But, in addition to her ministry as mother and homemaker, Judy's gift of interpersonal relationships provided another dimension of ministry within her circle of friends. She was someone to whom they could come to share the deepest concerns of their lives.

Third, it is clear that she was not being affirmed, equipped, and supported in her ministry. I certainly did not affirm or support what she was doing—I criticized her for putting up with all the problems of the neighborhood. Her church did not affirm or support her ministry because it was not done within the context of congregational life. And nowhere was she receiving help in equipping herself for a more effective ministry.

The ministry Judy was doing within the context of her primary role as mother and homemaker was a ministry of presence. She was present as an open and nonjudgmental person to whom others could go with comfort.

OUR PRESENCE IN THE WORLD

All of us have the potential for a Christian ministry of presence because we interact with others on a daily basis. In fact, people who work from 8:00 A.M. to 5:00 P.M. generally spend more of their waking hours with their workplace associates than with their families.

It is in the ministry of presence that the distinction between Christian and non-Christian actions can best be seen. In chapters 2 and 3 we talked about the ministry of competency. Yet competence is obviously not confined to Christians. In later chapters we will deal with ministries of ethics, change, and values. Yet there are many non-Christians who have high values, fine ethics, and work for constructive change. Similarly, there are many non-Christians who are open and nonjudgmental, and to whom people go with problems.

So then what is special about a so-called Christian ministry? Can't anyone do the kinds of ministry outlined in this book? The difference is fundamental and powerful. It has to do with this biblical principle of priesthood.

THE UNIVERSAL PRIESTHOOD

The role of the priest is to be the intermediary between God and other humans. The priest prays to God on behalf of others and the priest represents God to other humans. For most people the word "priest" usually conjures up the image of a Roman Catholic, Anglican, or Episcopal clergy person saying the Mass. Despite the Reformers' affirmations of a "universal priesthood" of the baptized, most Christians have great difficulty understanding that they are priests. The biblical evidence is strong, however, that all the people of God, both men and women, constitute a "kingdom of priests."

The identification of all God's people as priests first appears in the book of Exodus. In the third month after the Israelites had been led out of their captivity in Egypt, they set up camp at the foot of Mount Sinai. Moses went up the mountain to meet with God who gave him this message to deliver to all the Israelites:

> "You saw what I, the Lord, did to the Egyptians and how I carried you as an eagle carries her young on her wings, and brought you here to me. Now, if you will obey me and keep my covenant, you will be my own people. The whole earth is mine, but you will be my chosen people, a people dedicated to me alone, and you will serve me as priests." (Exodus 19:4–6 TEV)

We find no reference to just a select few being priests. The message from God was to *all* the people, men and women.

When the prophet Isaiah describes the future glory of Jerusalem, the people of God are to be known as "the priests of the Lord" (Isaiah 61:6a TEV). No qualifiers. No exceptions. All the people of God, men and women.

It is clear from the Old Testament that all God's people were called into a priestly relationship with God, not just a few.

Perhaps nowhere in the New Testament is the principle of a universal priesthood better set forth than in the first letter of Peter. The letter was addressed to all Christians scattered throughout the northern part of Asia Minor: "But you are the chosen race, the King's priests, the holy nation, God's own people, chosen to proclaim the wonderful acts of God, who called you out of darkness into his own marvelous light" (1 Peter 2:9 TEV).

The theme continues to the very last book of the Bible. The Revelation to John was again for the benefit of all God's people, not just the male religious leaders. In the salutation the author writes: "He loves us, and by his sacrificial death he has freed us from our sins, and made us a kingdom of priests to serve his God and Father" (Revelation 1:5–6 TEV).

These four examples of biblical references clearly indicate that God's people—that's us—are priests. It doesn't say that we try to be like priests; it says we *are* priests of the Lord. Nonbelievers, of course, make no such claim.

As intermediaries between God and humankind, we priests bring the concerns of the people to God through intercessory prayer, and we bring the concerns of God to the people by our words and deeds.

INTERCESSORY PRAYER

If we believe at all in the power of prayer, then we can immediately see how our priestly function of intercessory prayer can be a powerful aspect of our ministry. Intercessory prayer is not simply a way of calling to God's attention the needs of another person in the expectation that God will enter the situation and we can leave. Often we can be the channels for God's answer to our prayer.

This truth was vividly revealed to me some years ago when Judy and I were youth advisers in our little church in Detroit. The young people were questioning the power of intercessory prayer, and someone suggested that we try an experiment. The young people decided that they would all pray for something and see if God responded by acting on their prayers. They agreed that the prayer had to be for something that was verifiable, and they agreed that it would be for someone else, not themselves. Why not pray for those young people who had dropped away from the church since being confirmed, suggested one girl. They liked that idea, and each young person selected one absent friend for whom he or she would pray.

"Now we can't cheat on this experiment," one boy reminded the group. "Let's all promise that we will not let the person we're praying for know what we are doing." It was agreed.

A month later the youth group met to assess the results. They were shattered. Not a single one of those for whom they prayed had been seen in church during that month. One girl said she "thought" she saw her assigned girl in church one Sunday, but the others refuted her claim. The intercessory prayer experiment was a total failure.

Then Bob spoke up. "Something is wrong with this. I can't pray for Fred to come to church and see him every day in school and say nothing to him about my prayer. Why can't we say something to the person we're praying for?" There was a bit of debate over this request, but it was agreed that they all would continue the experiment for another month, and if they felt like telling their prayer partner about it, they could.

The following Sunday morning the youth choir was scheduled to sing. As the entrance hymn began and the choir moved down the aisle, I got a surprise I'll never forget. There was Bob and by his side, Fred, his prayer partner, who had not been in church for years!

Bob's immediate success encouraged a few others to be more open about their prayer experiment. As a result a few other young people returned to our church.

The young people's experiment taught me something about intercessory prayer. Each of them was in a position to *do* something about the request they were placing before God. It wasn't until they let God work *through* them instead of *for* them that their prayers were answered. It is true that there may be times when the person for whom we pray is so far removed from us geographically or by virtue of their condition of health that we cannot be the channel of

God's action. But we need to realize that many times intercessory prayer really is getting in touch with God in such a way that we become the channels of God's response to our prayer. When we pray to God on behalf of another person, we must always be prepared for the very likely possibility that God's reply will be, "Okay, I understand the need of your neighbor. You do, too. So how about you doing something about it, and my power will flow through you!" That is spirituality.

Intercessory prayer is the means by which the Christian approaches God on behalf of the people. That's one dimension of the priestly function. The priest is also a channel through which God approaches the people. This dimension is most readily seen when an ordained minister of the church preaches on the Word of God and administers the holy sacraments. But that priestly role applies just as well to laypeople in their daily lives. It is what I call the ministry of presence.

Each of us has a daily presence among many others. We are physically present in our families, in our jobs, in schoolrooms, and in our community activities. Since Christians affirm the omnipresence of God, we believe that the presence of God is wherever we are. This Godly presence can be made visible to others if we Christians permit God to work through us. That can be a bit tricky because we have to be open enough and subvert our own self-interest enough to permit God to act through us. But it can and does happen, as thousands of Christians throughout the ages have testified.

THE OFFICE EVANGELIST

Unfortunately, some Christians are so intent on being the channel of God's presence in the world that they set the agenda and write the scenario themselves. Helen was such a Christian.

Helen was the supervisor of about ten clerical people in one of the district sales offices of Bethlehem Steel. All the clerical people were in one large room, and Helen had a glass-enclosed private office in one corner of that room. On her desk was a Bible.

Helen was a born-again Christian and a faithful member of a church in our city. She was soft-spoken and very friendly. She really cared about people. It was her conviction that, as a Christian, it was her calling to bring the Word of God to others. She sincerely believed that the solution to any and all the problems of the world could be found in an appropriate quotation from the Bible.

And so it was that whenever she heard of any personal problems in the lives of the people she supervised, she invited them into her office, closed the door, and—in full view of everyone else—read the Bible to them. This was an unjust manipulation of employees by their supervisor; yet Helen did have a sincere interest in the problems of her workers, and regularly checked with them as to how things were going. Sometimes she invited them back to her office for prayer and additional Bible reading.

Most people avoided the uncomfortable experience of Bible reading and prayer in Helen's office by making sure no one knew of any of their personal problems. A few of them complained to me, because I was Helen's supervisor. I talked to her about what she was doing and suggested that she was unfairly using her supervisory position to advance her religious beliefs. She didn't see it that way. She honestly felt that God was calling her to help those with problems. I tried to point out that people actually were keeping their problems to themselves and laughing at her behind her back. That didn't bother Helen, because she believed that the world generally rejects the true Word of God.

Then she challenged me. She asked if it was not true that I was a Christian. I said that I was. She asked if I believed the words of Jesus when he said, "Go into all the world and preach the good news to all creation" (Mark 16:15 NIV). I said that I did. "Well, if you feel I'm doing it the wrong way, Bill," she said, "how are you doing it?"

That brought me up short. I explained that I tried to be an open person and held myself available to discuss any personal problem an employee had. If someone asked about my faith, I told her, I was willing to talk about it; but I didn't think it was proper for a supervisor to try to impose his or her religious beliefs on a worker. I knew I was kidding myself, even as I spoke. Few people felt I was an open person; most people were intimidated by me. And no one had ever asked me about my Christian faith.

I often tell people the story of Helen, and everyone wants to know what finally happened. I did two things. First, I made it very clear to Helen that I was happy that her faith was so important to her, but I disagreed with the way she was trying to share her faith with others. I told her that if it ever appeared that her witnessing was disrupting the work of her unit, she would have to discontinue it. Second, I gathered together all the people who worked under Helen, told them that they had the right to refuse to listen to her Bible reading, and promised them that I would do my best to insure that such refusals did not adversely affect their annual performance appraisals.

Some people always ask why I didn't flat out order Helen to stop her witnessing. I have a problem with that kind of action. Helen and her unit were being paid to do a job, and they were doing it well. Her witnessing did not seem to affect job performance any more than if she were taking an equal amount of an employee's time to talk about the previous night's television spectacular or her latest home-improvement project. A certain amount of socializing is appropriate with any supervisor-worker relationship, as long as the work does not suffer. It goes on in every office of every healthy organization. In Helen's case the topic of interest was her religion and the Bible. As long as people were free to turn away from her witnessing efforts, and as long as the work did not suffer, I felt it was unnecessary to insist that she cease all such conversation. I know that other business leaders may disagree with that position, but that's where I left it. Helen kept witnessing until the day she retired. Some people refused her requests; some went along with her, probably because she really was a kind and caring person. And the quality of her unit's work remained high.

Was Helen effectively fulfilling her priestly role of being the channel for God's action in her place of presence? At the risk of being judgmental, I think not. She was turning people off.

Unfortunately, many good, churchgoing Christians, while they dislike Helen's methods, have an uneasy feeling about their inability to witness to their faith. They do not feel comfortable in using biblical references or church language as they relate to others, yet they do not know how a Christian does go about bringing God's presence into a situation. Seldom do they get any help from their church. What their church should be saying to these people is that the priestly function is not restricted to such obvious religious acts as reading the Bible, saying prayers, and singing hymns. God's action through human form is much more expansive than that.

PRESENCE AMONG THE WOUNDED

My experience as a combat medic during World War II has allowed me to see a close analogy between what a medic does and the ministry of presence. Combat medics are not MDs; many of them have had no prior medical training. Yet without their work battle casualties would be enormous.

The combat medic is trained to determine if a battle injury is serious or minor. If the injury is serious, the medic is trained to take the steps necessary to keep the wounded soldier alive until he can receive the care of a professional doctor. If the injury is minor, the medic can treat it so that the soldier can return to action. Moreover, the medic must be very reassuring to the wounded. Combat itself is frightening; to be wounded in battle is terrifying. To have a friend providing help and assurance can go a long way in relieving the terror.

The ministry of presence is very much like the role of a combat medic. Although we're not in a war, we live in a world where people are being injured daily—physically, emotionally, spiritually. Do you know *anyone* who is not carrying some type of burden? All creation is filled with walking wounded. Then add to these real problems the fears they live with—fears about their future, their families, their health, their jobs, their self-worth. Fear can immobilize people.

Just as virtually anyone can become an effective medic, any Christian can effectively practice a ministry of presence. Some training is necessary, but the skills can be easily learned.

A LISTENING MINISTRY

One requirement of the combat medic is to be where the action is. Well, most of us already *are* where the action is—in our families, our jobs, our communities. Another requirement is to listen.

As a medic it wasn't enough to be where the action was; I needed to have my radio turned on. Without the radio in my jeep, I would not have heard the cries for help coming from burning tanks. It's the same in daily life: We need to listen. Unfortunately, we sometimes tune out the cries for help. Even if we are truly concerned and really stop to listen to the cares and concerns of another, we often fail to get the whole story.

Most of us are poor listeners. Since our mind moves forward faster than the words to which we are listening, we are frequently preparing something to say when we should be listening. That's one of my bad habits.

A part of the training program for our sales staff at Bethlehem Steel was a course in effective listening. Being a good listener requires certain skills. What a person says is not always what a person means. Body language can say a lot to the person who knows how to read it. We often need clarification and feedback in order to get the full and accurate message. Sometimes even the speaker is uncertain about how he or she feels.

Are we aware of our listening biases? Many of us tune out children or old people. For years many women have complained that men do not listen to them as carefully as they listen to other men. When we are angry about something, do we carefully listen to an explanation?

The world aches for good listeners. Many doctors report that they daily see patients who have nothing physically wrong with them. They merely need someone to listen to them. Other people go to the corner taproom and linger for hours over a few drinks, all the while talking to the bartender or a stranger on the next stool. Have you ever heard of a bartender being affirmed in his or her listening ministry by a member of the church? Just as the combat medic can patch up a simple injury and send a soldier back into action, so can an effective listener enable a person to continue with his or her daily life.

The listening ministry, all by itself, is a ministry of presence. Few churches ever consider helping their members improve their listening skills, so we may need to turn elsewhere for help. Packaged courses are available on effective listening, but they are generally slanted toward businesspeople. The best resource for self-study is a book, and two have been particularly helpful to me. They are *Listening as a Way of Becoming*, by Earl Koile, and *The Awesome Power of the Listening Ear*, by John Drakeford.[1] These books are not new, but their content is timeless.

REACHING OUT

Listening is one piece of the ministry of presence, and some-times listening is all that is required to meet the need. But at other times the need calls for an active response from us.

We used to see Joan and Carl each summer at our cottage com-munity in the Poconos. Then Carl developed cancer, and we watched him deteriorate over a period of years. Finally, one winter, he died. When we saw Joan the following summer, she talked at great length about how Carl died. She was very angry: None of their friends from church came to visit Carl, yet a group of Mennonites—strangers—came in once a week to do the house-cleaning for Joan and sing and play the piano for Carl. Joan loved these strangers for what they were doing for Carl, but she was in-furiated that their good church friends never showed up.

"Don't be angry, Carl told her in his last weeks of life. "They want to come, I'm sure, but they don't know what to say."

They don't know what to say.

How often have we passed up an urgent need to minister to the needs of another human being because we don't know what to do or say? What do we say or do when the loved one of a friend or coworker dies? What do we say or do if that person is in the process of dying? What do we say or do if a couple we have known closely for years begins divorce proceedings? What do we say or do if the child of a friend or coworker is picked up by the police for pushing drugs?

Mostly, we do nothing. We don't want to hurt the person more by doing or saying the "wrong thing." I know this to be true be-cause I have heard it expressed by hundreds of laypeople in work-shops when I have asked the above questions. Yet we all know that our friend or coworker is hurting and needs consolation and support.

Occasionally, when I ask people what they do when they come across friends who are hurting, someone will say, "I will tell the pastor about it."

Well, pastors do want to know about the needs of people in their own congregation, and most pastors do have the training and experience to say and do the appropriate ministering. But telling the pastor is not enough. We need to reach out ourselves.

As a medic my job was not simply to locate the wounded, radio the description of their injuries back to the surgeon at the battalion aid station, and then walk away from it all. No, my job was to provide assistance, the kind of assistance a physician might give in that combat situation. And the Army had seen to it that I received training from professionals to do the right things with battlefield wounds.

Why doesn't the Christian church use the same approach with the laity who daily minister in the world? Why don't pastors who are skilled in counseling take some time out to teach their laity some basic counseling skills? What do they say and do as they sit with men and women in grief? How do they relate to a couple going through divorce? How do they support the parents of a child who has gone wrong?

Furthermore, since most pastors who are skilled in counseling know when to refer a person who is in need of highly specialized help, why can't they help their laity to learn the signals of serious need? Just as the medic was trained to distinguish serious injury from simple injury, laypeople can be trained to spot the signals of people with very serious physical, emotional, or psychological problems and to get them to professional help quickly.

The Pastoral Care Team

This has happened in a somewhat limited way in our congregation. We call it the pastoral care team. About ten volunteers from the congregation plus the pastor and an outside licensed psychologist comprise the team.

The pastor is the intake person. When someone from the congregation comes to the pastor for counseling, he immediately determines whether he can meet the need or whether he should refer to the outside counselor. If he can meet the need, he follows through with the necessary hours of counseling. When that period is completed, he asks if the member would be willing to have two people from the pastoral care team do follow-up work. If the answer is yes, the pastor and two lay members of the team meet; and from that point on, visits are made by the lay volunteers, who regularly report back to the pastor.

If the pastor determines that the member needs more specialized counseling, he refers the member to the licensed psychologist. When the specialized counseling has been completed, the person is passed back to the pastor and then to a pair of lay volunteers on the team.

The pastor, the professional psychologist, and the lay volunteers on the team meet regularly to review all cases. The laypeople are coached in what they should say or do in response to certain events that may have occurred in connection with their follow-up visits.

Strict confidentiality is required for all members of the team. No one except the team members themselves and those they help know who is on the team.

The program has been effective. It has helped many people, and it has done one thing more: It has made good use of the talents of psychologist, pastor, and other caring people.

Basic Training for All

I recently noted with interest an article in *Modern Maturity* on "A Thoughtful Word, A Healing Touch."[2] It was an excellent article of "do's and don'ts" to observe when visiting gravely ill people, and it was drawn from the experience of people in Hospice programs. I was pleased to see AARP, the American Association of Retired Persons, reaching out to help people minister to others; but I was saddened by the realization that the Christian Education Committee of my congregation has never considered addressing this need.

Perhaps churches should begin to offer training to all members on some basic counseling skills. And while we're at it, let's offer courses on first aid, and CPR. A person with a working knowledge of first aid can literally keep someone alive until professional help arrives. Countless lives have been saved because someone on the scene of an accident knew how to administer CPR.

Adult church school courses in effective listening, basic counseling, and first aid? Does it sound wild? If so, it is one more example of how narrowly we look at the ministry of the whole people of God. For those who feel that education on Sunday morning should be restricted to Bible study, church doctrine, and theology, Jesus' words come through with sharpness: "Not everyone who says to me 'Lord, Lord,' will enter the kingdom of heaven, but only he who does the will of my Father who is in heaven" (Matthew 7:21 NIV).

By bringing into the educational programs of our churches some of the skills training that will help people minister to others in daily life, we will be helping Christians make the Monday connection.

Is it God's will that those who are hurting be ministered to? You better believe it. As we go about our daily lives, we need to keep open the way for God to work through us, and we need to be equipped with the skills to be effective priests of the Lord. That's the ministry of presence.

CHAPTER 5

The Need
for Grace

Claire has been in and out of our lives for many years. My wife, Judy, first met her during one of her visits to the local county prison, where Claire was serving a term for being an accomplice to armed robbery.

One of the driving forces in Judy's life has been Matthew 25:35–36: "I was hungry and you fed me, thirsty and you gave me a drink; I was a stranger and you received me in your home; naked and you clothed me; I was sick and you took care of me, in prison and you visited me." Judy's life has been dedicated to the literal expression of these words in her life, including years of work with and for those in prison.

Claire was a sweet, harmless, young woman whose major fault was that she seemed to be incapable of planning her life or considering the consequences of her actions. She got involved in the armed robbery because a boyfriend talked her into driving the car. During her parole period, she frequently missed appointments with the parole officer because she had agreed to go on a trip with friends a few days earlier. Judy spent hours trying to teach Claire to consider the consequences of her actions, but with little success. As a result Judy frequently found herself in the parole office with Claire, explaining her missed appointments and pleading for another chance.

Claire invited us to her wedding—the only nonfamily members to be there. We were a bit concerned because her new husband, Michael, also had a police record.

A few months after the wedding, Claire and Michael came to visit us. They needed help. They wanted to rent an apartment but did not have enough money for the deposit, and they could not get credit anywhere. Would we lend them $300 for a few months?

Judy agreed and we gave them a check.

For about six months we heard nothing from Claire and Michael. Judy called Claire's mother and discovered they had left town shortly after we gave them the money. Their whereabouts was unknown. We had been taken for $300.

Almost two years later we got a call from Claire. They were back in town, this time with a baby. Could they visit us? Judy said yes.

Claire and Michael were obviously glad to see us. They were back in town for good, they said, and Michael was about to start work next week. But they needed money. Could they borrow from us?

I reminded them that the first "loan" had never been repaid. They seemed surprised. Apparently, they had forgotten all about it. I looked at Judy and suggested that we needed to talk it over a bit. They left with our assurance that we'd let them know promptly.

Judy wanted to give them another chance; I was convinced we'd be taken a second time. I felt it was more realistic to consider the money as a gift than a loan, and were we really helping them by giving them more money? They certainly hadn't proved themselves to us.

So we hit upon a middle course. We decided to make a charitable gift to a local human services agency, whose director knew Claire and Michael. We asked the director to extend a loan to them and to follow up for payment. If Claire and Michael repaid the loan, the agency was ahead by $300; if there was a default, the agency was simply back to where it was before our gift.

Claire and Michael were very pleased with our decision. We learned later that they did not repay the loan.

Over the years Judy has helped Claire in other ways, but we have made it clear that there will be no more loans until they pay back the human services agency.

Is that the way Jesus would have done it? We're not so sure. It's hard to imagine him turning away a request even though the recipients are irresponsible. Would he continue to take a chance with Claire and Michael?

BE AS WISE AS SERPENTS

In the Gospel of Matthew we read the account of Jesus' instructions to the twelve disciples as he sent them out to preach the message, "heal the sick, raise the dead, cleanse those who have leprosy and drive out demons." He tells them to "give freely" because they have freely received. But in the midst of all this idealistic instruction-giving there is a warning: "I am sending you out like sheep among wolves. Therefore, be as wise as serpents and as innocent as doves" (Matthew 10:5–16 RSV).

Does this advice apply to the ministry of presence for today's disciples? I think so. But can we be both as wise as serpents and as innocent as doves? Isn't it one way or the other? I think not. To be innocent is not the opposite of being wise. The word "innocent" means to be free from guilt. It can also mean to be harmless in effect or intention. So Jesus is telling his disciples to use good judgment in their ministry, but not to become immobilized in trying to figure out what is the "right" action to take in an ambiguous situation. They are to act with the best of intentions and with the freedom to fail, without feeling guilty, if things turn out badly.

This is what Martin Luther was getting at when he wrote about sinning boldly. We are imperfect people. We do not have the infinite wisdom of God. Therefore, even with the very best of intentions, we are bound to make mistakes. Knowing that we are capable of making mistakes, we can do one of two things: We can study the problem forever and thus do nothing ("paralysis of analysis" is the business term). Or we can use the brains God gave us, make the best possible decision with the best of motives, and then act, knowing that God will not condemn us if we fail. We are innocent of God's judgment even before we act. That is sinning boldly.

If we are truly acting as an agent of God—a priest—then we have to trust that God's presence is with us. Jesus told his disciples not to worry about what to say if they are arrested. "At that time you will be given what to say, for it will not be you speaking, but the Spirit of your Father speaking through you" (Matthew 10:19–20 NIV).

RISK TAKING

The ministry of presence involves risk, good judgment, and the assurance of the forgiveness of God. Here too we see the similarity to the job of the combat medic.

There certainly is risk in being a combat medic, but it is not foolish or thoughtless risk. A dead medic is unable to help others. He must act, but he must also use good judgment with respect to personal safety. Then there is triage. Sometimes there are so many wounded that hard decisions have to be made as to whom to help first. Which ones will survive if I don't have time to help them? Which ones will die, no matter how much I help them? Which ones will live *only* if I help them? To seek out that third group in the confusion and terror of battle takes wisdom and courage. And sometimes you're wrong. But you go ahead, doing your best, using the skills you have been given.

The laity in ministry can perform a similar triage. We cannot help everyone. Some will survive without our help. Some will not survive despite our help. It is the third group that we need to discern: those who will survive because of our help.

But finding that group isn't as easy in daily life as it is in wartime. In combat the injuries, the needs, are apparent: bleeding, burns, compound fractures, shock. In our everyday world the injuries are not nearly as clear. Husbands and wives are not always able to communicate well with each other. Teenage children do not want to share their concerns with parents. Very few of us want to reveal our weaknesses, particularly in a work environment in which competition is a way of life.

I have found this to be a real obstacle to a ministry of presence as a manager. It's all very well for managers to say that they have a genuine interest in their people and that they maintain an open door so that employees can share their problems with them. I think we managers delude ourselves.

Consider this: In most organizations it is the manager who makes recommendations for merit increases or bonuses or promotions. Employees who are eager to advance naturally want to appear to be capable, self-confident, and able to deal with problems, especially in the eyes of their manager but also as seen by their peers. If I am vying for a promotion, am I going to let my manager know about a physical condition I just developed that could be potentially life threatening? Will I tell my manager that I am worried to death about my teenage son who is on drugs? Will I reveal that my marriage is breaking up?

In my long career as a sales manager, precious few employees took advantage of my "open door" to share a personal problem. I confess that I have not been very effective in my ministry of presence, but I think that most managers share my struggles to be open and nonjudgmental in an environment where everything is judged.

One way to deal with this problem is to seek the help of an assistant or associate. At Bethlehem Steel I relied upon my secretary to be my eyes and ears for employee problems. Shirley developed her own interoffice network and was able to keep me advised of the problems and hurts among our employees. But even with this help it was difficult. I could not risk the employees knowing what she and I were doing or else the network would shut down. At best I could arrange to have a work-related conference with an employee who reportedly had a personal problem and, through the way I directed questions, give the employee every opportunity to share the need voluntarily.

I feel it is important not to enter a person's private life unless invited. People are entitled to their privacy. Yet it has been especially painful to be working with and supervising an employee whom you know is hurting badly but who chooses to keep the pain inside.

This brings up one of the most difficult problems for the ministry of presence: how to bring the theology of grace into a world of works.

THE THEOLOGY OF GRACE

One of the fundamental principles of the Christian faith is that God's love and concern extends to all people, without respect to how well they behave. When Jesus instructs his followers on the need to love one's enemies, "so that you may be sons of your Father who is in heaven," he reminds them, "for he makes his sun rise on the evil and on the good, and sends rain on the just and on the unjust" (Matthew 5:45 RSV).

Christians are defined by their relationships to God, not by their good works. If I accept God's relationship with me as revealed through the life, death, and resurrection of Jesus Christ, I am a Christian. If I do not accept that relationship, no matter how good my life may be, I am not a Christian.

Does this mean that a Christian need not be concerned with doing good deeds? Not at all. But the good deeds come as a result of accepting the assurance of God's acceptance of us. A person who lives in full and certain knowledge of God's free gift of grace cannot help but be moved to do good works. In Matthew 7:17–20 Jesus uses the analogy of the fruit tree. A good, healthy tree naturally produces good fruit. Good fruit does not make the tree healthy; it is the result of the status or condition of the tree. Therefore Jesus can say, "By their fruits you shall know them."

This doctrine of justification by faith through grace is one of the three primary affirmations of the Reformation (the other two being the authority of the Bible and the universal priesthood of the baptized). The realization of this doctrine was a conversion experience for Martin Luther. As a young monk Luther struggled to be good enough to be certain of God's acceptance of him. Yet, no matter what he did, he remained uncertain of his worthiness. It was during a reading of St. Paul's letter to the Romans that the answer came to him: "For we hold that a man is justified by faith apart from works of law" (Romans 3:28 RSV). It was then that Luther realized that it was God's action, not his, which assured his everlasting relationship with his creator. He later wrote of this moment, "Then I had the feeling that straight away I was born again and had entered through open doors into paradise itself."[1]

The principle of justification by faith through the grace of God is particularly difficult for us to believe in today's society, for it is diametrically opposed to our everyday experiences. In the eyes of the world, we are identified by what we do and our worth is determined by how well we do it.

THE WORLD OF WORKS

What is the first question that usually surfaces when two male strangers introduce themselves to each other and exchange their names? It is either, "What do you do?" or, "Where do you work?" Male identity is established by the work they do; and with an increased number of females in the work force, more females establish their identity the same way. Very seldom does a man initially ask another male stranger a question that has to do with relationships, such as, "Who are your parents?" or "Are you married?" or "Do you have children?"

Although female introductions are more likely to deal with questions of relationships, I have frequently heard one woman ask another, "What does your husband do?" For many years some women's identities were established by their husband's occupation: "She's the president's wife," or "Her husband owns a hardware store."

Have you ever taken a good look at the birth and death announcements in your local newspaper? They reveal an interesting difference in emphasis. Birth announcements always deal with relationships: "A daughter was born to Mr. and Mrs. John Doe." Obituaries, on the other hand, always deal with work first and relationships last. My local paper, for example, lists two obituaries: "Dr. Martin R. Corning, retired podiatrist" and "Anna May Carter, taught in Coplay and Allentown." After listing the life achievements of both the deceased, family relationships are noted. But work comes first.

Most of us know of people who have had a very difficult time moving into retirement. One of our close friends, in contemplating retirement, said, "All my life I have been a chemist. When I retire, I will be nothing." Many people have serious emotional problems when they lose a job, because their jobs have been their lives. During the severe downsizing of the steel industry in the 1980s, large numbers of people in our community were laid off. Even though it was not their fault that they had lost their jobs, they took it hard. Many of them went into deep depression; drug and alcohol use picked up; and there were increased cases of child and spouse abuse.

Clearly, then, our identity is largely established by what we do and our worth by how well we do it. We keep score by accumulating wealth, power, and prestige. If I do well, I will get a raise or a promotion or a company award. The public will know I am worth something when they see the kind of car I drive or the size of my home or the academic degrees behind my name.

Our competitive society even goes to work on our children with this "theology" of works. Our grandsons tell me about their achievements in Little League. Our granddaughter, Amy, wants us to see how well she can ride a horse in competition. Kids compete in all kinds of contests, and the winners are more esteemed—have greater "worth"—than the losers.

Yet the theology of grace says that in the eyes of God, no one is of greater value than another. All are assured of God's acceptance, without regard to how well they do in life.

The theology of grace is a wonderful, liberating principle. The theology of works is a deadly, enslaving concept.

The ministry of presence calls us to bring the theology of grace into the world of works. Why? Because the theology of works grinds people down, but the theology of grace lifts them up.

To bring the theology of grace into a world of works, however, is perhaps the most difficult challenge facing a Christian today. I'm not sure if many of our clergy appreciate the difficulty, as they preach on witnessing to our faith.

Our Monday Connection breakfasts have proved to be an excellent place to wrestle with the issue of communicating a theology of grace in a world of works. For example, at one session, a member told of his problems with an employee who had been promoted to a position beyond his abilities by a previous manager. The employee kept trying, kept failing, and kept asking for another chance. "How many times should I give this person another chance?" asks the presenter of the case. "When I fail and ask for God's forgiveness, I'm assured of another chance, am I not? Shouldn't I treat others the same way?"

On another occasion a supervisor told of one of her employees who is a workaholic and a perfectionist. "She is very uptight," said the supervisor. "She works long hours, and her work is virtually perfect. But at the least hint of criticism from anyone, she gets very upset. She's not a happy person. On the one hand, I want to affirm her good work; but on the other hand, I'd like to help her see that there is more to life than one's job. How can I do both?"

"I have the same problem, except it is my boss who is the workaholic," chimed in another participant. "He works long hours overtime and has created an atmosphere in which everyone feels pressured to do the same. His family life is on the rocks and I'm concerned about what he is doing to the rest of us. How do you talk to your boss about life being more than the job? Or should we all look around for other jobs?"

These are all difficult questions. How can we resolve the wrenching dilemmas that come with a ministry of presence?

It seems to me that if we are to be God's agents in the world, we need to keep every avenue open for discerning God's will in a given situation. That's spirituality. One avenue is a good knowledge of God as revealed through the Scriptures. Unlike Helen, who read the Bible to troubled employees, I do not feel the Bible has a specific prescription for every problem we face. But the theme of justice in the Old Testament and the theme of love in the New Testament do play out in a variety of specific stories that may offer us some guidance.

A second avenue is the way in which God speaks to us through others. That's why Christian support groups are absolutely critical for the ministry of laypersons. As we share decisions and dilemmas among God's people, there is reason to believe that God's will can be discovered. Jesus told his disciples, "For where two or three are gathered in my name, there am I in the midst of them" (Matthew 18:20 RSV). Although God sometimes speaks to us through our clergy, both through sermons and through individual counseling, we must not place unfair expectations upon our clergy to solve complex work-related problems. The clergy do not have enough experience in many work-related fields to offer the kind of options that surface when the problems are shared with a peer group of committed Christians. On the other hand, many clergy have good experience with family-related or interpersonal problems.

Finally, I think we have to believe that, in some mysterious way, God does literally act through us. St. Paul referred to many of his acts by claiming, "It is no longer I who live; but it is Christ who lives in me" (Galatians 2:20 TEV). Similarly, Jesus told his followers that the Spirit of God would speak through them (Mark 13:11b TEV). At a few points in my life, as I reflect upon them, I behaved outside of my normal pattern in meeting the needs of another.

For example, I'm not the type of person to sit down and make a list of those who might be lonely or in need of a friendly visit. I'm too busy with the tasks of the day. If I hear of a friend who needs help, I'll respond; but I don't usually search out the lonely. A few years ago, however, I happened to think of an old teacher I had in high school, Mr. Neeley. He had to be almost ninety, I thought, if he was still alive. For some reason I felt a need to check and acted on it. His name was still in the phone book, and my call yielded an invitation to visit him.

A few nights later I found myself in his dimly lit living room. He was very feeble. His wife made us some coffee as we reminisced about the days at Allentown High School. I thanked him for being such a good teacher. As I was leaving, he took my hand and thanked me profusely for coming.

Three weeks later I read of his death. His wife called me after the funeral to say that I was the only one of his former students who had visited him in more than fifteen years. "He didn't feel so lonely after your visit," she said.

This experience taught me a valuable lesson. If I can press myself to lay aside my own agendas in order to let God's will flow into my thoughts, I will discover ministries that otherwise never would have occurred to me. It doesn't happen often, but when it does, it's exciting.

The ministry of presence is not my strong suit. I have been too much of a controlling person to provide space for Jesus to be within me. My controlling nature has diminished with age, but I still fight the battle of surrendering my will to God's.

We can give thanks for those brothers and sisters in the faith who are living in a large measure of surrender to Jesus Christ in their lives. The ministry of presence is a special spiritual gift these men and women can share with all of us.

IV

ETHICS

CHAPTER 6

A Crisis in Ethics

Historians may look back on the 1980s as the decade of America's crisis in ethics. Government, business, sports, and even religion saw steady streams of resignations, indictments, convictions, and jail terms resulting from ethical improprieties, many of which were illegal.

More than one hundred top officials of the Reagan Administration were charged with unethical activities. National Security Adviser Richard Allen resigned amid controversy over a $1,000 gift he received for arranging a special interview with Nancy Reagan. Anne Burford, EPA Administrator, resigned after disclosures that she bent environmental regulations for certain industrial polluters. Michael Deaver, Deputy White House Chief of Staff, was indicted for perjury, resigned, and was later convicted for violating federal conflict of interest laws. Guy Fiske, Deputy Secretary of Commerce, resigned amid charges of conflict of interest in contract negotiations. John Horton, Assistant EPA Administrator, was fired for using government employees for his personal business. Rita Lavelle, EPA Assistant Administrator for toxic wastes, was convicted of perjury concerning preferential treatment for a former employer. White House aide Lyn Nofziger was convicted of violating federal conflict of interest laws. Peter Voss, Postal Service Governor, pleaded guilty to charges of expense account fraud and accepting kickbacks.[1] On the Democratic side of the Congress, House Speaker Jim Wright resigned amid charges of violating congressional ethics and possibly federal law.

Commenting on the scandals in Washington, nationally syndicated columnist Robert Wagman writes, "The prevailing view of political ethics during the Reagan administration has been: If they can't send you to jail for it, then it's ethical."[2] This was the position taken by Edwin Meese, the nation's top law enforcement official, after Special Counsel James McKay decided not to prosecute him on several indictable matters because it would be too difficult to prove that he had the required "criminal intent" necessary to get a conviction.[3]

"Washington has become an ethical swamp," writes Fred Wertheimer, President of Common Cause. "Our nation's capital is addicted to special-interest influence money, and members of Congress are benefiting professionally and personally from these funds." He adds, "We've always experienced individual cases of corruption and impropriety in government. But today we have a system of institutionalized corruption. The rules themselves allow activities to take place legally that are improper and corrupting."[4]

The business world was equally shaken, as prominent leaders were exposed for unethical and illegal actions. Ivan Boesky, dean of Wall Street arbitrageurs, was sentenced for up to five years in prison for insider trading. Jacob Butcher, prominent Tennessee banker, was given a twenty-year prison sentence for bank fraud. Aldo Gucci, the patriarch of an international fashion empire, pleaded guilty to tax evasion. Dennis Levine, a prominent investment banker, was sent to jail for stock fraud. Paul Thayer, former chairman of LTV Corporation, was sent to prison for his role in an insider trading scheme. E. Robert Wallach, personal friend of former Attorney General Ed Meese, was convicted of racketeering and fraud in the same Wedtech scandal for which Mr. Meese claims to have been exonerated.

Other corporate leaders have gone to prison for such crimes as sending employees to their deaths in highly toxic plants, knowingly marketing tainted baby food, and willfully violating environmental laws. The federal government and big business were jointly involved in a huge Department of Defense scandal, in which some of the largest corporations in the country were accused of defrauding the Pentagon—with the help of government employees.

Sports saw its share of ethical problems. An Olympic gold medal winner had his award taken away when it was discovered he used steroids in violation of the rules. A number of colleges, including the two largest ones in Oklahoma, were punished for football recruiting violations. In professional baseball a popular national hero, Pete Rose, found himself tossed out of the sport due to gambling charges.

Several highly popular television evangelists were found to be diverting money into their own pockets, participating in sexual misconduct, and cheating on their income taxes. Richard Dortch, aide to TV evangelist Jim Bakker, pleaded guilty to mail fraud, wire fraud, and conspiracy, charges that could keep him in prison for ten years. Bakker himself got a forty-five-year term.

While it is the misdeeds of well-known public personalities that grab the headlines, ethical misconduct was also revealed among many middle-level and lower-level managers. Surprisingly, many of them received no personal gain from their misdeeds; they were merely trying to help their company or their division look better.

THE FALLOUT

A decade of unethical and illegal scandals has taken a toll on the nation. The general public has become very cynical about our system. Trust in politicians, government employees, and business-people is very low. Despite the fact that a number of high-profile personalities have gone to prison, the belief is still voiced that if you're poor and black and steal $50, you go to jail; but if you're rich and white and steal $500,000, you can beat the rap.

The scandals have made ethics a hot topic in America. Colleges and universities that have never offered courses in business ethics before are now doing so. Books and articles on ethics abound. Professional associations are giving more attention to their ethical standards through articles in their journals and workshops at their conventions. Ethics has become a growth industry in the 1990s.

The issues of justice, love, concern for the other person and stewardship of all creation are fundamental principles of the Christian faith. But we must remember that good deeds do not define the Christian faith; they flow out of our faith. Therefore, in expressing faith in daily life, Christians should be vitally concerned about ethics. All Christians have a ministry of ethics. Unfortunately, too many Christians have expressed such simplistic formulas as, "If you are right with God, you will be right with the world," or "The

Ten Commandments and the Golden Rule are the only ethical codes we need." Those notions ignore the fact that we live in a very complex world in which the interests of different groups are often at odds with each other, and there are frequently no simple solutions. A ministry of ethical decision making involves an intentional approach to the resolution of complex problems.

FIVE MISCONCEPTIONS ABOUT ETHICS

Before we can discuss the way in which Christians can carry out their ministries of ethics, we need to clear up five common misconceptions about ethics. These misconceptions concern the definition of ethics, the question of whether ethics can be taught, the idea that good people make good decisions, the question of legislating morality, and the leader's responsibility for the ethics of the group.

Defining Ethics

First, we are much too fuzzy about the meaning of the term "ethics." We tend to use the words "ethics," "values," and "morals" interchangeably.

A *value* is a worth or merit we place upon a particular thing or action. We value life, for instance. Our *morals*, on the other hand, are the principles we adopt with respect to right or wrong conduct. Because we value life, for instance, we adopt principles of conduct that aim to preserve life. The system of moral principles we adopt is our *ethics*. Because we value life, we support life-preserving principles and then work out a system—the ethics, if you will, for applying those principles in given situations.

For example, I value human life. My moral principles tell me that it is "wrong" to take a human life and "right" to save a human life. But what do I do when I am confronted with a situation where a deranged killer is about to take the life of a third party and I can save that life only by taking the life of the killer? The ethical system I have worked out says that if there is no other option that will save the life of the third party than to slay the killer, I will do so.

Why did I arrive at this decision? Well, there are other moral principles at play that help shape my action. For one, it is "wrong" for an innocent person to be harmed. For another, it is "right" that society be protected from deranged killers. Ethics, then, is the system for applying the various moral principles of my life to given situations.

Teaching Ethics

The muddiness surrounding the meaning of ethics leads to the second misconception shared by many people: You cannot teach people ethics. Felix G. Rohatyn, the well-known financier who is credited with saving New York City from bankruptcy, wrote this about ethics: "I no more believe that ethics can be taught past the age of ten than I believe in the teaching of so-called creative writing. There are some things you are born with, or they are taught by your parents, your priest or your grade school teacher. But not in college or graduate school."[5] I disagree.

I suspect that what Rohatyn meant to say is that a person's values are quite well set by the age of ten. I happen to disagree with that statement also. For example, many white children in South Africa value the life of a black person less than that of a white. Does Rohatyn believe, therefore, that it is impossible for any white South African over the age of ten to change and value all lives equally? But, assuming that Rohatyn knew the meaning of the word ethics, I most certainly disagree with the notion that we cannot teach people to make ethical decisions. Ethics is not some single quality that people have or don't have; ethics refers to making decisions when numerous, and sometimes conflicting, moral principles are involved.

Paul Thayer, former chief executive officer of LTV Corporation, was sentenced to four years in prison for stock fraud. He takes strong exception to the myth that you can't teach ethics. Reflecting on his own situation, he said, "Most of us have a child's notion of ethics and a graduate school notion of finance, marketing and management."[6]

Do Good People Always Make Good Decisions?

A third misconception is that "good people make good decisions." That is, people with good moral principles will naturally act in the right way. Or, to put it negatively, "bad" decisions always trace back to people with poor moral principles. That's just not so. First, in order to make an ethical decision, one must have all the relevant facts. If a good, moral person is making a decision without all the relevant facts at hand, it is quite possible that the result will be a bad one. A good example of this misconception can be seen in the controversy surrounding the *Challenger* space shuttle accident.

The generally accepted cause of the accident was the inadequate design of the O-rings that sealed shut the various segments of the huge fuel cylinders attached to the space shuttle itself. Investigators later discovered that one engineer in the department responsible for the production of the fuel cylinders at Morton-Thiocol had expressed concern about the adequacy of the O-ring design. But there was apparently no indication from previous flights or from plant tests that the design presented an undue risk.

NASA had also determined that a space launch should not occur at temperatures below freezing. At the time of launch, the temperature was above freezing, although technicians at the launch pad were concerned that some ice was still on the equipment. It was later felt that the combination of the low temperature and the questionable O-ring design created a situation in which the fuel escaped through the joints and was ignited by the flames from the rocket engines. Would the launch have occurred if those who made the decision had heard firsthand from the technicians concerned about residual ice? One can only speculate. But the people responsible for the launch did not have access to those concerns.

The shuttle tragedy did not occur because immoral people knowingly risked the lives of the crew. It occurred because the reporting system did not work properly and not all the facts were known.

It is in this area of collecting all relevant data that church leaders can often be criticized as they speak "prophetically" about the problems of our times. It is so easy to make sweeping generalizations about very complex issues and arrive at a flawed moral judgment. "Corporate greed," for example, is not the engine that drives all companies; therefore, if a wrongful act of a company is to be criticized, "corporate greed" should not automatically be labeled as the cause.

Another reality that calls into question the notion that "good people make good decisions" is that the end result of a decision involving a variety of factors cannot be determined with accuracy ahead of time. In the rush to find a drug that will be effective in treating AIDS, researchers have had to take some risks. Rather than do long term, exhaustive tests for side effects of potential remedies, they are following a shorter process. If it later turns out that more lives have been lost due to side effects of the drug than were apparently saved by its effectiveness, was the decision to make it available an unethical one? Were the decision makers immoral?

Hindsight is always 20–20. It is easy for church leaders and social moralists to condemn the actions of people who did what they thought was right, not knowing how it would all turn out.

Legislating Morality

The fourth misconception has been around for a long time: "You can't legislate morality." The experience with Prohibition in the 1930s is cited as proof positive. What is overlooked, however, are the numerous instances when morality has been successfully legislated. The morality of giving women the right to vote was legislated. Slavery has been eliminated. Social Security for the elderly, unemployment insurance, worker's compensation, safe working conditions, equal employment opportunity, nondiscrimination in schooling, housing, and jobs, and countless other matters that reflect the values and morality of a nation have become part of our legal code.

These laws certainly have influenced the behavior of the population; but have they actually changed the morality of the public? I think so. The system in which I was raised as a child accepted a variety of forms of discrimination as natural. Blacks "naturally" had dirty and menial jobs. Women "naturally" were paid less for the same jobs as men. Disabled people "naturally" could not go to the same places and do the same things as the rest of us. The establishment of a wide range of laws prohibiting discrimination has helped to shape my moral principles. I would now be outraged to live in a society where the kind of discrimination exists that was once so invisible to me.

The Responsibility of the Leader

A final misconception that needs to be shattered is the belief that the leader of an organization is ultimately responsible for the ethics of all those within the organization. It is true that the leader must have high moral standards and the leader must try to get others to act in accordance with those standards. But it is not correct to assume that the leader can always do so.

Organizations have cultures, and these cultures do not change overnight. During my time as manager of sales at Bethlehem Steel, we got a new chairman who had a sincere concern for the plight of black people. At that time there were no blacks in management positions. In the steel plants the blacks invariably had the dirtiest, most dangerous jobs. Our new code of ethics, which we had to sign, prohibited discrimination. The chairman sent us periodic letters regarding the need for affirmative action. Frequently, such letters were discussed in the managers' dining room with a good deal of joking. "Is the old man kidding?" someone would chuckle. "No, he's just doing this to paper the files," was the usual response. The word "nigger" was still commonly heard throughout the organization, and blacks continued to be the butts of most of the jokes. It took perhaps fifteen years for the corporate culture to change to what the new chairman was working for when he first stepped into his new job.

If wrongdoing is uncovered in a major corporation, it may be unfair to lay the blame on the present CEO. It may be more a reflection of the morality of previous leadership. Corporate cultures change slowly.

Ethics Codes

Formal codes of ethics are hot items these days. Profit and nonprofit corporations, trade associations and professional societies, are scrambling to adopt or refine codes of ethics. It is wise to maintain a degree of skepticism regarding the extent to which a code of ethics can ensure ethical performance within an organization. One thing is certain: Any organization that requires all its employees to review and sign its ethics code each year, and then does nothing else to encourage high moral behavior, is wasting its time on the code.

One of the shortcomings of any code of ethics is the problem of scope. A short, readable code of ethics will only cover broad areas of activity. One that tries to cover all areas of behavior will be so long and detailed that no one will read it.

William Frederick, a business professor at the University of Pittsburgh, has done extensive studies of corporate codes of ethics. One of his findings is startling: "Corporations with codes of ethics are cited by federal agencies for infractions more often than those that lack such standards."[7]

Why? Because most corporate ethics codes typically emphasize items that will tend to improve profitability. "The codes are really dealing with infractions against the corporation, rather than illegalities on behalf of the corporation," says Marilyn Cash Mathews, a Washington State University researcher.[8] Her studies of 202 corporate codes of conduct revealed that rules regarding relations with the US government were mentioned 87 percent of the time. Customer/supplier relations were mentioned 86 percent of the time. Political contributions were dealt with in 85 percent of the codes; and conflicts of interest showed up in 75 percent of them. All these items are important in keeping the corporation out of trouble. On the other hand, items concerning the company's role as a good citizen seldom are addressed. For example, only 25 percent of the codes studied included the corporation's civic and community responsibilities. Only 21 percent mentioned product quality, and only 9 percent spoke of product safety. Only 13 percent mentioned environmental affairs. Finally, only 6 percent dealt with personal character matters, such as the treatment of fellow employees.

A code of ethics that does not relate to the reality of the corporate culture is meaningless. It is nonsense to talk about equal opportunity in an ethics code when any employee can see that women and minorities are concentrated in low-paying jobs and top management is largely composed of graduates from the same university.

At Bethlehem Steel I reviewed and signed a code of ethics once a year. Once or twice a year, someone from the law department gave us a lecture on the antitrust laws—but not on ethics. Twelve times a year—once a month—I received a detailed profit-and-loss statement for each of the thirty shops and mills for which I had a responsibility. And I could usually expect to receive a request from my senior vice president for a written explanation of why the least profitable of the facilities wasn't doing better. Mind you, it wasn't

always a matter of *losing* money at a particular plant, it was about
making *more* money. Now what is a corporation saying to an employee when once a year there is a code of ethics to sign and twelve
times a year there must be an accounting for profitability?

I'm not against profits. A business corporation must make a
profit or it dies. The point is that if a company is really serious about
ethical behavior, it must pay more attention to achieving it. Some
companies have corporate ethicists, who review top corporate decisions. But what about decisions at lower levels? Some companies
have ombudsmen, to whom employees can go with their ethical
concerns. Chemical Bank of New York offers classes in ethics to employees, using actual case studies as material for their courses.

I believe that any company that has periodic performance appraisals should include items relating to ethical behavior. For example, employees should be reviewed regarding how they treat
coworkers and how helpful they are to others. Supervisors should
be rated on how accessible they are to employees and customers,
how well they listen to complaints, how much they encourage employee participation in decisions, and how much they seek feedback from employees.

THE ROLE OF CHURCHES

US churches have tried to play a role in the formation of better
corporate ethics. In a number of cities church, civic, and corporate
representatives have come together to form an organization specif-
ically dealing with corporate ethics. One of the best known is New
York City's Trinity Center for Ethics and Corporate Policy, an outreach ministry of Trinity Church, located in the financial district of
lower Manhattan.[9] It offers courses for executives and regularly
holds luncheons to discuss business ethics. Its advisory council
consists of business leaders, business school professors and ethicists, and church representatives.

The Center for Ethics and Corporate Policy in Chicago is a similar coalition of church, business, and academic representatives,
offering consultative services, seminars, and forums.[10] Other centers, which do not have a specific religious connection, can be found
in Boston; Washington, DC; Tempe, Arizona; Newark, Delaware;
and Charlottesville, Virginia.

In recent years various religious denominations have used the leverage of their pension funds to address moral issues in corporations in which they hold stock. The single most important issue for a number of years has been the presence of US corporations in South Africa. Many denominations have taken the position that, by staying in South Africa, American corporations are helping to prop up a morally repugnant system of apartheid. They have been filing shareholder resolutions for many years, urging management to leave South Africa.

The Interfaith Center on Corporate Responsibility in New York is a clearinghouse for those denominations that are active players in the corporate social responsibility movement.[11] In addition to the South African issue, ICCR members deal with equal employment issues, the environment, the world debt crisis, pharmaceutical marketing, military production, nuclear power, plant closings, and similar issues. As a member of the board of directors of ICCR for six years, I can testify to the fact that shareholder action can bring about some change in corporate behavior. Although ICCR members are frequently seen as adversaries of the corporations, in a number of instances corporate management has thanked the religious representatives for bringing up an issue the corporation had ignored.

Church representatives bring with them a genuine passion for justice and high ethical standards. Too frequently, however, they project an air of moral superiority, which can get in the way of solving ethical problems. Church representatives are also sometimes prone to making sweeping moral judgments without getting all the facts.

Our lives connect in many ways with large institutions, and our ministry of ethics involves a number of responsibilities. First, we need to observe the ethical behavior of our institutions. Then, if we have some misgivings, we need to raise the awkward questions. When we encounter an ethical problem, we owe it to ourselves and others to get all the relevant facts and to go through the process of ethical evaluation described in the next chapter. If it is clear that an ethical problem exists, we then need to determine the role we can play in bringing about change. (The ministry of change is explored in chapters 7 and 9.)

Jesus was frequently challenged by the Pharisees on the issue of obeying the laws of the Scriptures. Because he violated some of those laws, such as the strict observance of the Sabbath, he was accused of blasphemy. He denied that he had come to do away with the Jewish laws. Instead, he said, "A new commandment I give to you, that you love one another" (John 13:34 RSV). He demonstrated this principle when, out of love for a man with a withered arm, he healed him on the Sabbath, an act that was forbidden by the strict interpretation of Jewish law.

So it is with us. The commandments and moral principles we receive from the Bible cannot cover every possible ethical situation. But Jesus' overall law of love is the foundation of all ethical decision making. By keeping that principle in mind, we introduce Jesus into our ethical decision making. There must be a spirituality of ethical decision making. This is the ministry of ethics.

CHAPTER 7

Decisions, Decisions!

When we make ethical decisions, we must consider three factors: utilitarianism, rights, and justice. First, we must respect the interests of those who will most be affected and seek that action which will have the greatest utility for all. At the same time we must respect the rights of individuals. Finally, the decision must be fair or just. Although this may seem straightforward, sometimes the three tests of utilitarianism, rights, and justice suggest differing actions. The following case study illustrates in detail the nature of ethical decision making.

At one of our Monday Connection breakfasts, Carl told us of a dilemma he was facing. About six months earlier Carl, a real estate agent, had purchased the second half of a twin home as an investment. He felt that the house was in an area of town where it would appreciate in value. At the time he purchased it, there was a tenant paying $600 a month rent. Carl's monthly payment to the bank was $1,000 per month, but he considered the $400 difference his investment for the future. He wrote a letter to the tenant, advising that he was the new owner and that the lease would be continued at the same rent. He received one month's rent. The second month's rent did not come in. After several notices yielded no rent, Carl went to see the tenant.

The tenant turned out to be a woman with three young children who had recently been deserted by her husband. She had no marketable skills, but had secured a job as a check-out clerk in a supermarket. However, after she paid for child care and food, there was not enough money left for rent. She said she was unable to locate her husband, but asked for a bit of time. No rent came in the third month, and only a $25 payment arrived in the fourth month. Carl again visited with the woman to discuss some options. He learned that the woman had parents living in Florida who had helped her out of an earlier financial bind. But the woman said that she did not want to go to her parents again, because they had warned her about her husband in the first place. She had no other resources.

Carl summed up his situation this way: "I have already paid the bank $6,000 on my investment and I have received only $625 out of $3,600 due. I see no prospects for a quick change in the situation. As a Christian, what do you think I should do?"

The group offered Carl several options: Evict the family. Locate and contact her parents in Florida. Sue the man who sold you the house in the first place. Try to sell the house without revealing to the buyer the problem of nonpayment of rent. Let her stay and take your losses. Have her go to the local Council of Churches for emergency housing assistance. Help her try to locate her husband and take legal action against him.

As our group discussed various options, it was clear that they were considering the problem in the light of three different approaches: utilitarianism, rights, and justice. Let's look at these more closely.

UTILITARIANISM

The utilitarian principle is based on doing the most good for the most people or the least harm to the fewest people. It calls for a complete listing of alternative actions. For each alternative action there must be an assessment of all the benefits derived from that action and all the detriments associated with it. That alternative action which has the greatest net benefits, after subtracting the detriments, is the most moral action to take.

The utilitarian principle requires us to consider all the stakeholders, that is, everyone who will be affected by any of the alternative actions. In Carl's situation we identified the following stakeholders: Carl; the woman and her children; Carl's other employees (in the event he should be forced into bankruptcy); the woman's family in Florida; the bank; the missing husband; the man who sold Carl the house; the Council of Churches; and a potential new buyer of the house. Not all stakeholders had the same degree of interest in the problem, but all had to be considered in following the utilitarian principle.

A Christian can support the utilitarian approach to decision making because it causes one to be concerned about all stakeholders. It does say that we are our brother's keeper. It does move us in the direction of good stewardship.

There are some problems connected with the utilitarian approach, however. One problem is how to measure the benefits and costs of various actions for the various stakeholders. Is the $600 rent more important to the woman than to Carl? If so, how much more? The woman would be very upset if Carl went to her parents in Florida, but how do we measure her displeasure against Carl's $600 per month rental income? How can we measure the emotional distress of evicting the woman and her children? There are times when the utilitarian approach serves very well as a decision making process, but it has shortcomings and needs to be checked against the other approaches of rights and justice.

RIGHTS

Rights are that which is due to anyone by just claim, legal guarantees, or moral principles. Rights are that to which one is entitled. There are two general types of rights: legal rights and moral rights.

Legal rights are those guaranteed by virtue of law. The US Constitution contains a Bill of Rights that guarantees every US citizen such rights as freedom of speech, assembly, religious expression, and so on. We have a body of law that deals with commercial issues such as contract rights. Legal rights differ from one jurisdiction to another. For example, a woman's rights to her deceased husband's property may vary from one state to another.

Legal rights come into play with Carl's situation. Since a lease is a legal agreement, Carl has the legal right to his $600 a month rent; if he does not get it, he has a legal right to take action against his tenant. If Carl feels that the man who sold him the house knowingly did not tell him the problem with the tenant, he may legally sue for misrepresentation of facts in the sale. If he is considering selling the house to someone else, the buyer also has a legal right to know all the circumstances connected with the sale. Carl cannot legally mislead the buyer, because the buyer's rights must be protected.

Moral rights are entitlements that are not necessarily guaranteed by law, but which are generally accepted as being due to all people. These rights are frequently called "human rights." Human rights are universal and, unlike legal rights, do not change with jurisdictions. They are entitlements for every human being to do something or to have something done for them.

In December 1948 the United Nations General Assembly adopted a Universal Declaration of Human Rights, which all nations on earth are encouraged to teach and observe. The preamble of the Declaration states that "recognition of the inherent dignity and of the equal and unalienable rights of all members of the human family is the foundation of freedom, justice and peace in the world."[1]

"Freedom," "justice," and "peace" are good biblical words. So much so that the American Bible Society produced a little booklet in 1976, *Life in All Its Fullness: The Word of God and Human Rights,* in which the thirty articles of the Universal Declaration of Human Rights are given biblical foundations.

"Biblical history is freedom history," reads the study guide. "To be created in the image of God is to be given the gift of freedom and the awesome responsibility that goes with that gift. Our true identity and full potential can only be realized in freedom."[2]

Moral rights are not one-way streets. If I am entitled to certain rights as a human being, then I also have the "awesome responsibility" of making certain I extend those same rights to others.

What are the rights contained in the thirty Articles of the United Nations' Universal Declaration of Human Rights? Many of them will be familiar to Americans, who live in a nation where there are extensive legal guarantees of human rights. The right to "life, liberty, and security of person" is presented in Article 3. The right to "freedom of thought, conscience, and religion" is contained in Article 18; while Article 19 states the "right to freedom of opinion and expression." Articles 5 through 11 deal with legal rights relating to the judicial system, all of which are guaranteed to US citizens.[3]

There are some rights listed which we, in the United States, support as moral rights, but which are not fully guaranteed to us by law. For example, Article 25 states,

> Everyone has the right to a standard of living adequate for the health and well-being of himself and his family, including food, clothing, housing, medical care, necessary social services, and the right to security in the event of unemployment, sickness, disability, widowhood, old age or other lack of livelihood in circumstances beyond his control.[4]

Our Social Security system, unemployment, and welfare programs do guarantee some of the above needs to some of our citizens. But 40 million Americans are without any form of health insurance, and millions have no permanent housing.

In defense of this reality, some Americans will say that we provide the opportunity for anyone to have health insurance and housing if he or she is willing to work. That's fine individualism, but it ignores some basic facts: In 1987 there were 32.5 million Americans living below the poverty level. Twenty percent of all children born today are born into poverty. Children cannot get jobs. While the condition of the elderly has improved in recent years, there are still millions of people living in poverty who are too old to work. There are many too disabled to work. Finally, millions of American citizens work very hard and are still in poverty. For instance, 12.6 percent of all farm people were living in poverty in 1987.[5] Commenting on the increasing rate of poverty during the 1980s, Robert Fersh of the nonprofit Food Research and Action Center said, "The 1980's have been a terrible decade for the poor in America despite overall progress in unemployment and the economy."[6]

Article 25 raises the question of what America should do about those who, for reasons beyond their control, cannot attain an adequate standard of living.

Article 23 deals with the right of everyone to have a job. We all support this moral right, but it is another right that we do not guarantee by law.

Most of us would agree with Article 14, which states that every human being should have the right to leave his or her country for reasons of political, religious, ethics or similar forms of persecution. Yet we have very strict limitations on the numbers of people who can enter this country as a result of such treatment.

If we consider Carl's options in the light of moral rights, several items come to our attention. The tenant and her children do have a human right to housing (although they have no legal right to stay in Carl's house without paying rent). Carl needs to consider the woman's right to privacy if he plans to contact her parents contrary to her wishes. On the other hand, Carl has a right to earn a living at his job and to feed, clothe, and shelter his family.

Using the method of reviewing rights to make an ethical decision presents some problems, just as the utilitarian approach did. If two rights are in conflict, how do we decide which right is more important? Is the woman's moral right to have housing more important than Carl's legal right to evict her for nonpayment of rent? People will answer that question in differing ways, based on their own moral principles.

How do rights relate to utilitarian options? If Carl were to decide, on the basis of the utilitarian standard, that his best option is to contact the woman's family in Florida, does her moral right to privacy eliminate this option? Although people will differ on this question, it is generally true that moral rights have greater weight in decision making than do utilitarian approaches.

JUSTICE

The third standard we should apply to ethical decision making is justice. The word "justice" is usually defined as the administration of a legal system. Here, however, justice means fairness: to conform to generally accepted standards of right and wrong in matters affecting people who could be wronged or unduly favored.

Standards of justice generally are considered to be more important than utilitarian considerations. If Carl is considering an option that is highly desirable from a utilitarian standpoint, but it is unjust or unfair, he probably should scrap it. For example, is it fair to evict a woman and her children when she is doing everything she can to keep her family going?

With respect to justice, the United Nations' Universal Declaration of Human Rights says, "Justice is required in human relations and in the ordering of social structures, not because we thereby prove ourselves worthy by acts of justice, but because we are responding gratefully to our oneness in creation and our oneness in Christ."[7]

The United Nations study guide points out that peace is possible only where there is justice, and says this about peace: "Peace involves reconciliation, trust, and wholeness. Wholeness, i.e., life lived in integrity, security, and realization of human potential, is possible only in a loving, forgiving, accepting community of persons, where the value of personhood has priority over that of property, race or social status."[8]

Manuel Velasquez, in his textbook on business ethics, speaks of three types of justice: distributive, retributive, and compensatory. Distributive justice is concerned with the fair distribution of society's benefits and burdens. A capitalist view of distributive justice would be, "Benefits should be distributed according to the contribution each individual makes to achieving the aims of his or her group." A socialist approach to distributive justice would be, "Work burdens should be distributed according to people's abilities, and benefits should be distributed according to people's needs."[9]

THE CHURCHES ON DISTRIBUTIVE JUSTICE

In recent years several religious denominations have issued statements on economic justice that deal directly with the issue of distributive justice. In 1980 the Lutheran Church in America, at its biennial convention in Seattle, Washington, approved a social statement entitled, "Economic Justice: Stewardship of Creation in Human Community."[10] I was privileged to play a small part in the design of that statement.

The US Roman Catholic Bishops took six years of consultations and rewrites before the third and final draft of their paper, "Economic Justice for All: Catholic Social Teaching and the US Economy," appeared in June 1986.[11] I provided some testimony for this paper in a review consultation in July 1984.

In January 1987 the United Church of Christ published a study paper on "Christian Faith and Economic Life."[12] The Presbyterian Church (USA) published its own paper, "Christian Faith and Economic Justice," for study in its congregations.[13]

In all four cases heated debate arose over the way distributive justice was being viewed. Because all four papers dealt with the needs of people in our economic system, conservatives within the denomination claimed the papers were socialistic in tone. The feeling was expressed that the notion "from each according to one's abilities and to each according to one's needs" was a call for a larger welfare system. While the denominational statements were careful not to condemn the capitalistic system, they did insist that any economic system must be judged on "what it does for people, what it does to people and how people participate in it," to use the language of the Roman Catholic document.[14]

As a businessperson and management consultant, I support the principle that workers should be rewarded according to the contribution they make to their company. But there are some limitations to that principle. First, it is very difficult to measure accurately the degree to which any worker contributes to the organization. Second, do salaries go up and down from year to year based solely on someone's judgment of individual contributions? Bonus incentives, yes, but salaries? Many salaries are set more by what the market pays for a particular job than by what the individual workers contribute to the company. So the capitalist system of distributive justice does not really exist in a pure form.

But, as a businessperson and a Christian, I also think our economic system must consider the needs of people. Our "right" to a decent standard of living must be fulfilled. Whether it is fulfilled by the private sector or the public sector can be debated, but it must be fulfilled. Until our nation finds a way to meet the needs of 32.5 million of its citizens living in poverty, we have no right to gloat over the apparent collapse of communism as an economic system.

Velasquez defines retributive justice as "the just imposition of punishments and penalties upon those who do wrong."[15] If I steal from you, I must pay a penalty.

Compensatory justice, according to Velasquez, "concerns the justice of restoring to a person what the person lost when he or she was wronged by someone else."[16] I carry automobile insurance so that if I damage the property of another person, they can be paid for it.

As we apply the standards of justice to Carl's situation, several points emerge: A socialist view of distributive justice would suggest that the woman's needs override her lack of contribution to the rent; the capitalist view would ignore her needs. Which view should prevail here? Certainly, the option involving the Council of Churches would relate to socialist justice, since the Council is offering housing assistance without any contribution on the part of the tenant. Retributive justice could come into play if Carl sues the former

owner, or tries to sell the house to another person through decep-
tion. Compensatory justice would be the result if Carl could locate
the missing husband and force him to pay all the back rent.

As the breakfast group discussed the ethical decision Carl had
to make, differences of opinion emerged regarding his options.
There seemed to be a general agreement on two points: First, the
woman and her children needed housing. Carl could not just put
her out on the street. If he ultimately had to evict her, he would
have to help her find affordable housing.

Second, Carl could not let the present condition continue indefinitely. He had a right to his money, and it was not fair that he
should pay because of what the woman's husband did. The group
was evenly split about trying to contact the parents in Florida.
While most saw the Council of Churches housing fund as a possible
temporary measure, one person objected on the basis that the fund
was for people who had no other resources, and Carl could afford
to forego the rent for a while longer. All agreed that it would be
wrong to sell the property deceitfully, but one or two suggested
there might be a difference between outright falsehood and perhaps revealing only the information that a prospective buyer might
request. There was a general agreement that trying to help find the
missing husband and then forcing him to pay might cost too much
and have no certainty of success (an instance where a utilitarian
view was preferred to the compensatory justice consideration).

In the end the group consensus was that Carl should employ
a combination of options, with some being held in reserve in case
the first steps fail. But it was clear to all that it was up to Carl to make
his own ethical decision. We would support him with our prayers.

SITUATION ETHICS AND COMPROMISE

In my conference work on ethics with various Christian groups,
I have encountered two misconceptions: "Situation ethics is
wrong" is the first, and "Christians must never compromise" is the
other. Both statements need to be thought through.

Apparently, many people have the idea that situation ethics
means that you have no set moral values, but just design them in
each particular situation. "Do whatever feels right" is the way one
man explained his understanding of situation ethics. I have heard

more than one sermon in which situation ethics was described as un-Christian. Nonsense.

Situation ethics means that we must first have an established body of moral principles and values. Then we look at each situation and apply the various moral principles in an effort to arrive at a decision. This is what our Monday Connection group did with Carl's dilemma. Then, if it appears that the best moral decision involves ignoring one moral principle so that a conflicting moral principle can work, I ignore that principle *in this specific situation*. Repeating the illustration cited earlier, I highly value honesty and always want to tell the truth. I also value human life highly. If the only way to save the life of a third party from a deranged killer is to tell the killer a lie about where the third party is hiding, I would do so without question. Does that mean I now no longer value honesty? Not at all. I will continue to be a truth teller.

If I were faced with Carl's dilemma, I would highly respect the woman's right to privacy, because privacy is an element of personal dignity. Therefore, if I were Carl, I would not contact the woman's family in Florida against her wishes. I would try other options first. But if everything else failed and there was nothing left but eviction or losing money indefinitely, I'd go back to the woman and try to persuade her to go to her parents. I might even tell her that she must either go to them for help or face eviction. In this situation, I would try all other approaches before laying aside my value of the right to privacy; but, in the end, I'd pressure her to see it my way. Some will disagree with my approach, but it does describe situation ethics.

"Christians must never compromise" raises essentially the same issue. In order to function without ever compromising our moral principles, we have to construct a list of principles rigidly arranged in descending order of importance. What goes at the top? Don't say "love," because love is manifested in a variety of ways. Is "preservation of life" highest, or is "truth telling" at the top? Peter denied Christ three times out of fear of losing his life. Would you do the same?

There are several accounts in the New Testament where Jesus compromised on the religious laws of his day. Harvesting grain on the Sabbath was one such prohibition. Yet he permitted his disciples to pluck some heads of grain as they were walking through a field on the Sabbath. When criticized by the Pharisees, he defended his action by stating that the Sabbath was made for man, not man for the Sabbath (Mark 2:23–28).

On another Sabbath, in a synagogue, Jesus challenged the Pharisees on their strict absolutes. Pointing to a man with a withered arm, he asked, "Is it lawful on the sabbath to do good or to do harm, to save life or to kill?" (Mark 3:4 RSV). Answering his own question, since he knew they were plotting to accuse him, he healed the man. Straightaway the Pharisees went away to report another of Jesus' compromises.

Was Jesus discarding the laws of his faith? He said not. "Think not that I have come to abolish the law and the prophets; I have come not to abolish them but to fulfil them" (Matthew 5:17 RSV).

Then what was he getting at? He was intent on having people break away from the stifling rigidity of law that permits no compromise.

When the Pharisees again tried to trick him by asking which was the greatest law, he replied "You shall love the Lord your God with all your heart, and with all your soul, and with all your mind. This is the great and first commandment. And the second is like it, You shall love your neighbor as yourself. On these two commandments depend all the law and the prophets" (Matthew 22:37–40 RSV). He repeated the same message to his disciples at the Last Supper. "A new commandment I give to you, that you love one another; even as I have loved you, that you also love one another" (John 13:34 RSV).

The commandment to love is much too broad to codify into rigid "do's" and "don'ts." So how, then, are we to love? Jesus tells his disciples that they are to love one another, "even as I have loved you." The style of Jesus is the way. It is a style that is flexible in seeking out the most loving action in a given situation. It is not a rigidly structured list of moral imperatives. It is a style that may, at times, set aside a commonly accepted moral principle if the situation requires it in order to express love. In short, we can only carry out the law of love if we are open to situation ethics.

We form most of our basic values early in life, and our family is a powerful force in shaping them. Values by themselves, however, are only the building blocks of ethical decision making. We must arrange our values in a way that they will meet the requirements of a particular ethical situation. To use the three standards of utilitarianism, rights, and justice is one approach to applying values to a complex problem such as that faced by Carl. It is the way in which we go about our ethical decision making that ultimately makes a difference.

The process of ethical decision making can be learned. It is unfortunate that so many people have simply assumed that good values make for good people and good people make good decisions.

The ministry of ethics requires us to have some knowledge of how to relate our values to complicated situations. Here again is a subject that should be and rarely is offered in Christian education programs in our churches. In the complex world in which we live, there is indeed a call for Christian ministry in ethics.

V
CHANGE

CHAPTER 8

The Courage to Change

It was ten o'clock in the morning of my first day in my new job as manager of sales. Ten o'clock was my usual time for a stretch and a cup of coffee, so I asked my secretary for the directions to the room where the departmental coffee pot was brewing.

"Oh, Mr. Diehl," said my secretary, "I'll get your coffee for you."

"No thanks, Shirley, I'd prefer to get it myself."

"But I got it for the previous manager," she insisted.

"Well, that's fine, but I think I'll get my own coffee."

"I get it for your three assistant managers," she continued, undaunted.

"Shirley, I don't think your job description includes getting coffee for the men in this department. You are a professional and should be treated as one. If you feel that you should be getting coffee for my assistants, it's up to you. I just want you to know that you are not expected to wait on me."

I chuckled to myself as I wandered down the hall toward the coffee room. I knew my wife and three daughters would have been proud to have observed one of my first management decisions. Living with a houseful of feminists does cause one to rethink one's traditional ways of doing things.

I continued to get my own coffee and I began to notice that, one by one, my assistant managers were getting their own coffee also. The practice spread, and before long every man in that department was getting his own coffee. I later heard from other managers in the company that we were known as "the department where everyone gets his own coffee."

When I tell that story among business people, someone will occasionally comment that the manager's time is too valuable to waste in getting coffee, and that a good manager will delegate such a menial task to a lower paid employee. To which I respond, "Baloney!" Managers waste all kinds of time talking about golf or the weekend football games or in prolonged phone conversations. Besides, as Peters and Waterman have pointed out in their best seller, *In Search of Excellence,* there is great benefit in "managing by walking around."[1] I tell those who disagree with my practice of getting my own coffee that it enables me to manage by walking around. That shuts them up.

Another incident happened shortly after I became manager of sales. At a private party in Bethlehem, I ran into one of my former professors at Lehigh. He congratulated me on my promotion and then asked, "What are you going to do with those other managers at Bethlehem Steel to get the company to clean up the air and water in this town?"

"Nothing," I replied.

"Nothing?" he asked with astonishment. "Don't you care that the air around here is polluted and that the shad can't even live in the Lehigh River anymore?"

"Certainly I care about it, and so do the other managers I've talked to. No one likes pollution. But you asked what I am going to do to get our management to correct the problem. I'm telling you there is nothing I can do about it."

"Afraid to rock the boat?" he challenged.

"No, I'm just being realistic," I responded. "Look, it will cost hundreds of millions of dollars to clean up the water and air around all our steel plants. We are in a very competitive market. The company is not going to spend hundreds of millions of dollars on pollution control equipment while our competitors are spending hundreds of millions on equipment that will lower their production costs or improve their quality so that they can beat out our brains in the marketplace. Unless every steel company cleans up their environment, none of them will. I think legislation is the only way it will happen. That way everyone will have to do it, and we'll all be in the same boat. Frankly, I do send money to those organizations trying to get environmental laws into place, and I hope you are doing the same."

Our nation and our state did enact demanding environmental laws a few years later, which forced the entire US steel industry to clean up the air and water. Today the air in Bethlehem is free of pollutants, and shad are again taken from the Lehigh River each spring. The city of Pittsburgh is a dramatic example of how legislation changed the environment of an entire region. It is true that some steel management fought such legislation, and that some marginally productive plants were closed because the cost of cleaning them up could not be justified from an economic standpoint. No major change comes without some pain. But no one in the steel industry today would want to have us return to the days of polluting the air and water around us.

A PRAYER ABOUT CHANGE

As manager of sales, I was in a position to directly change the way women were treated in our department, but I was not in a position to directly change the way our company was polluting our community. In both instances change was necessary and change did come about, although my role was quite different in each. In these situations I was reminded of a well-known prayer of Reinhold Niebuhr, sometimes known as the Serenity Prayer, which has long been one of my favorites: "O God, grant us the serenity to accept what cannot be changed, the courage to change what can be changed and the wisdom to know the difference."[2]

We live in an imperfect society. The litany of the kinds of problems which need to be addressed is long indeed.

God cares passionately about the welfare of all creation. If there is to be constructive change in our world, those of us who see our roles as priests of the Lord need to be the channels of God's acting for the benefit of creation. We need to be change agents for God. Most assuredly, there is a ministry of change and, in one way or another, each Christian can participate in it.

Christians can be faulted for too often following the first part of the Niebuhr prayer, that is, seeking the serenity of accepting things they cannot change. More to the point, perhaps, they can be faulted for their image of what it means to be "peaceful." Don't be contentious, don't disagree, don't challenge authority. These are the marks of peacefulness in the eyes of many Christians. Yet the Bible is filled with the stories of God's people in contention with the way things were, in disagreement with commonly accepted practices, and challenging the authority of others. Jesus was such a person. His death was brought about by the religious leaders of his day, who could not tolerate his ministry of change.

Christians can also be criticized for not having the courage to change the things they can. Far too often we overrate the kinds of consequences that may result from our efforts, and we underrate the kind of support we may get from others who share our concerns but are also afraid to act.

A few years ago I served as a consultant to the former Lutheran Church in America in its corporate social responsibility work. Because the pension funds of the church were invested in the stocks of many large American corporations, we had a shareholder's right to question management on some of its policies. I went into many management consultations to raise questions about corporate policy in such areas as environmental concerns, plant closings, business in South Africa, equal employment opportunity, sex discrimination, and the like.

Generally, the meetings were cordial but very cool. Corporate management was not receptive to criticism from church groups. I came to expect defensiveness and argumentation whenever I entered the corporate conference room.

Every now and then, however, I was surprised. I distinctly recall being escorted to the lobby by a senior executive of a major corporation after a rather heated consultation on the company's practices on waste disposal. When we were alone, he said, "I want to thank you for what you said in that conference room. I have been concerned about our waste disposal practices for years, but I lacked the courage to bring it up. Now that you have opened the door for discussion, I think I have an opening to bring about change."

Such reactions were admittedly few, but they did happen often enough to give me courage in facing some hostile corporate leaders.

TRIAGE AND CHANGE

The final element of the Niebuhr prayer is for the wisdom to know the difference between the things we cannot change and those we can. As a former combat medic, I am drawn to the principle of triage when I look to those areas where my efforts are needed for change. Certain problems, such as the tremendous population explosion in India, I am helpless to change. Other problems are being attended to by many others, and probably will be resolved without my personal involvement. For instance, much effort has been directed at the war on cancer in our nation. Other than an occasional contribution to the American Cancer Society, any extra effort I put into this cause will have little significant effect.

However, there is that third group of problems requiring change for which one may have special talents to contribute or for which a critical mass of support is needed in order to resolve the issue. For example, for some reason I do not fully understand, there are not many Christians—lay or clergy—speaking out on the critical need to connect faith to daily life in relevant ways. I have felt called to use my experiences in the church and in the world to lift up this issue, which is badly in need of change. That is the only reason why I am writing this book.

Judy and I applied the triage principle to our involvement in the Vietnam War issue. Initially, I believed our nation's objectives and policies in Vietnam were correct. Our children and their friends did not. As our daughter and son protested the war on their college campuses and in Washington, DC, we sat on the sidelines, uncertain about what the answer to it all was. But then came Kent State, and we saw the television coverage of American troops killing American students on American soil. Judy and I decided that only the participation of middle-agers such as us in those demonstrations would cause our nation to reconsider its policy. And so we began marching in Allentown and Harrisburg and Washington.

My business associates thought I was crazy, but a critical mass of people was needed to cause a reevaluation of our presence in Vietnam. We persuaded other adults to join us, and noticed that older people had joined the protests all across the country. Before long the nature of the protest had changed. Americans of all ages were marching in the streets. The tragedy of Vietnam soon came to an end.

The tricky thing about triage is having "the wisdom to know the difference," as the prayer says. Much too often our "wisdom" tells us that there is nothing we can do. But every now and then someone surprises us.

Terry Rakolta, a suburban Detroit housewife and mother of four, catapulted to national attention in early 1989 when she wrote to complain to the chairmen of five companies that were sponsors of a television program she found offensive for family viewing. She let the *New York Times* know what she was doing, and happened to get her story on the front page of one of its issues. That put her in the national spotlight and won her a number of appearances on network television programs.

Ms. Rakolta insists she is not a censor. She says she finds a great inconsistency between a company's television commercials and the programs they sponsor. "My argument is that if these giant megacorporations really loved your family, they would say, 'Buy our products because they are used in the best interests of your family.' But the next time you turn on the TV you see soft-core pornography, people talking about oral sex, people talking about doing it with animals, and they're sponsoring it!"[3] She rebuts the "just turn off the television" and "parents should control the use of TV" arguments by pointing out that 50 percent of American women work and are not always present to monitor what their children see.

Following the nationwide exposure of Ms. Rakolta's views, some sponsors withdrew support of the offensive program. The network that aired the program and the agency that sold advertising for it denied, however, that her criticism had anything to do with the sponsors' actions. I wonder.

I do not tell this story to debate the merits of what Ms. Rakolta did, but simply to illustrate that time and circumstance may cause the efforts of one person to have an effect far beyond what that person could have imagined when he or she first set out to advocate change. Ms. Rakolta acknowledged this reality when she said in one of her interviews, "I must have just pressed the right buttons."

When Rosa Parks, tired after a long day's work, refused to go to the back of the bus in Montgomery, Alabama, she had no idea that she was striking the first spark of a nationwide civil rights movement. Time and circumstance were right.

Although we must use wisdom in the triage process of determining where we apply our energies and talents for change, we should not discard the possibility that God may be giving us a wild card to play, and that time and circumstance may be ripe for us to bring about greater change than the best wisdom could ever have predicted.

FORCE FIELD ANALYSIS

One of the most helpful ways to assess the possibility of bringing about change is through the use of the force field analysis, originated by Kurt Lewin.[4] Step one is to define exactly what kind of change is desired.

For example, let's assume you work for a company that employs about five hundred people. Your supervisor frequently makes derogatory statements about women, calls them "Hon" or "Babe," occasionally pats one of them on the rear end, and asks women to run errands for him, which men are never asked to do. Your objective for change is clear: to have the supervisor discontinue his sexual harassment.

Now ask yourself whether you are in a position to cause that to happen. Make two columns on a sheet of paper. In one column list the forces that work against having your supervisor change his style: He has never been reprimanded by management. There is no written company policy against sexual harassment. The other men in the department laugh at his jokes and take no exception to what he is doing. It is possible that he has never been confronted with how women feel about his style. None of the other women in the department have complained. In the other column list the forces that work in favor of having the supervisor change his ways: Sexual harassment lawsuits generally receive sympathetic treatment in the courts today. Some of his practices could be in violation of Title VII of the Civil Rights Act of 1964. Some of the men in the department seem to be respectful of women in other ways. Top management in the company generally appears to be considerate of employees and acts ethically.

If you want to bring about change, the forces in favor of change have to outweigh the forces against change. Look at your list. Can some of the forces against change be eliminated or changed into forces for change, and can some of the forces for change be strengthened?

The answer is yes, the forces can be changed. Next question: Are you in a position to make these forces change? Probably, yes. How? You could start a lawsuit against the company, but that is a high-risk step to take. That may be your action of last resort, but meanwhile there may be other possibilities.

Is there a way in which the threat of such a lawsuit could come to the attention of top management? An anonymous letter to the president? The intervention of a lawyer friend talking to the company's lawyer? Is there a way in which you or a group of the women could request a written code on sexual harassment be drawn up by management? Can some of the men in the department become advocates for change? Is there a way in which your supervisor's boss can be approached on the matter?

Use of the force field analysis enables us to determine the possibilities for change, the strategies for change, and the role that we will have to play in making it happen. It also gets us away from the idea that people who oppose the change are "enemies." That is a mistake made by many who are too simplistic in their approach to change. If we remember that most people act out of self-interest, the task of change is to find ways in which it is in the interest of those opposed to it to support it.

Change can be initiated from within an organization, or it can be initiated from without. In the instance of who gets the coffee in the office, change could be initiated from within the organization since I held virtually all the cards. It would not have been nearly as successful had I been an assistant manager and my boss insisted on the secretary getting his coffee. In the instance of pollution of the air and water around a steel plant, change had to be initiated from outside the organization.

In both cases the change is facilitated if forces both within and without the organization favor it. The women's movement, a force external to my department, certainly was aligned with what I was doing with respect to the coffee situation. Because of this I feel sure the other men in the department were somewhat prepared for what I did. Similarly, since there were people within the company who had a concern about the environment of our plants, the external force of legislation that caused us to change enabled them to express their concerns and to make suggestions for implementation. Change comes about best when forces both internal and external to the institution are working for it.

POWER

Use of the force field diagram implies two things Christians frequently eschew: the use of power and the nature of institutions. We can hear it expressed with the words, "Christians use love to persuade, not power," and "If there are good people in an institution, it will be good." Both statements need rebuttal.

As Christians we recognize the power of God and the power of Jesus. We talk of the power of evil in the world. Why do we have trouble with the thought that we should use power in service to God? Jesus clearly gave power to his followers for ministry on his behalf. "Jesus called the twelve disciples together and gave them power and authority to drive out all demons and to cure diseases" (Luke 9:1 TEV). The Apostle Paul reminds the early church of the power they have received through Jesus. "To him who by means of his power working in us is able to do so much more than we can ever ask for, or even think of, to God be the glory in the church and in Christ Jesus for all time, forever and ever! Amen" (Ephesians 3:20–21 TEV).

In *Money, Sex and Power* Richard J. Foster points out that there are various types of power. The love of power, like the love of money, can destroy us. Just as we can use money in fulfillment of God's purposes, so can we use God's power flowing through us. It is not our power; it is God's power. Foster writes, "Of all people, spiritual people know the dangers of power. The temptations to abuse are everywhere. Yet we must not back away. Christ calls us to the ministry of power. He will give us the compassion and humility to fulfill our ministry."[5]

THE NATURE OF INSTITUTIONS

In our discussion of ethics, we saw that, within institutions, it is possible for good people—working with the best of intentions—to make decisions that turn out to be bad. If we are to have a ministry of change, we must recognize the nature of institutions, because so much of what goes on in our world is shaped by institutions.

Institutions take on a life and culture of their own that can shape the lives of those who work within them. When I entered high school, I found a culture awaiting me. I adopted the dress code and social patterns of the group. We had a tradition to uphold. We did not choose our chief sports rivals; they were passed along to us by tradition. It was more important to beat Bethlehem in football and Hazleton in basketball than any other teams, because they were our traditional "enemies."

A similar culture awaited me at college. The traditions and practices of the past had much to do with the practices of the present. When I began my working career with Bethlehem Steel, an even stronger culture awaited me. It was a culture in which I was expected to conform in the way I dressed, the way I perceived economics and the role of government, the distrust I should have in unions, and the social habits I adopted. I felt subtle pressures to live in certain parts of town, support the Republican Party, play golf as my sport of choice, read certain newspapers and magazines, and share common world views.

Churches are prime examples of how institutions pass their cultures along to their members and shape their behavior. Despite the rhetoric of a "oneness in Christ," denominations have vastly different views on such basic things as baptism, the inerrancy of Scripture, the doctrine of ministry, and the locus of authority. I find it impossible to explain to a non-Lutheran why I cannot receive Holy Communion in a congregation of the Lutheran Church-Missouri Synod, or why members of the Wisconsin Synod will leave the room when prayer is offered by someone who is not a member of their branch of Lutheranism. If we put religion aside, these people are very fine, likable, caring human beings. But their institution has shaped their behavior so as to exclude me from it unless I adopt its culture.

In *Moral Man and Immoral Society* Reinhold Niebuhr points out that the institutions of society are likely to be more sinful than the people who make them up.[6] He speaks of the "brutal character" of organizations and reminds us that whereas humans do have a moral potential, institutions do not. The nature and character of the institution can shape the behavior of those individuals who interact with it. The power to possess and control people is demonic. The institutions of society, our corporations, our schools and colleges, our governmental units, our volunteer agencies, and our churches can be demonic.

The Apostle Paul makes reference to "principalities and powers" in his epistles (Ephesians 6:12 RSV). It is clear he is not talking about individuals, but rather such "dominions" and "authorities" that exercise control over people.

William Stringfellow argues that demonic principalities and

powers also include such ideologies as capitalism, socialism, astrology, humanism, scientism, and patriotism.[7] He says that we are incredibly naive to assume that the principalities and powers are benign. They are not. Frequently, they are out to dominate and control humans.

Therefore, since institutions are directly or indirectly involved in everything we do today, and since they can be demonic in nature, those who work for change must be well aware of the character and culture of those institutions they would seek to change. It would be a great mistake to assume that all we need to do to change the direction of an institution is to change the direction of its leader.

In my work as a management consultant, I frequently come across instances of sex, race, or age discrimination within my client organizations. Each time, the president of the company has been shocked with the discovery. He will produce company policy statements or letters he has written to all employees. I have never doubted that these men are sincere in their beliefs. The problem lies in the fact that a culture that has discriminated against women, minorities, and the elderly for many years does not change overnight just because the chief executive of the organization wants it to happen. It takes time and effort to change the culture of an institution.

Why are there not more women in top positions of corporate America? In the 1970s the explanation was that it took time to climb the corporate ladder, and women were too new and too few to the business community. Today that explanation is not persuasive. While women make up about 40 percent of the demographic category of managers and administrators in America, less than one-half of 1 percent are among the top officers and directors of American business. From 1978 to 1990 the number of officers and directors of Fortune 500 companies who are women grew from ten to only nineteen.[8]

The problem is that the culture of American business is so heavily imbued with male practices and life-styles that it is extremely difficult for women to fit in. Even ignoring the issue of women taking time off for childbearing, the fact remains that women who do not have children encounter subtle barriers in the male-dominated culture of American business.

"Corporate males still don't know how to deal with women. They are afraid to yell at them or to give them negative feedback," says Ellie Raynolds, a partner at Ward Howell International, an executive recruiting firm. "Men often worry women will run from the room in tears, or, worse yet, yell back."[9] It may take another decade or two before women's competency is recognized and rewarded the same as for men; but, for the sake of justice, the culture must change.

Because of this nature of organizations and the complex structure of our society, bringing about change means that frequently we must be political in our strategy and tactics. Some Christians have trouble with this thought. "Be prophetic!" is the cry of those who choose not to get involved in the stickiness of political action. The role of the prophet is important, but change will not come simply because the need for it is pointed out by someone who stands on the sidelines. More about political tactics in the next chapter.

ACT LOCALLY

As we examine our ministry of change, it is important to "think globally and act locally." The scourge of drugs facing our nation and many other nations is one of global dimensions. Yet it is quite clear that it cannot be eradicated by any act or acts that our government may take. We must fight the war on drugs on every level, local as well as national. The problems of homelessness, poverty, child abuse, and racism may also seem overwhelming when considered as a whole. Yet, if we have the opportunity to deal with them on a local level, we should not be deterred by the enormity of these problems. We act locally.

The United States is one of the most powerful and influential nations in the world; but our leaders are elected by people acting locally. We live in a nation where at least once a year we are asked to vote for people who will lead our institutions of government and for propositions that will change our patterns of civil life together. Many elections, including presidential ones, could have gone the other way if there had been a shift of just a few votes in key districts. When Christians do not vote, they abdicate their ministry of change.

From the opportunity to vote and play a part in governmental change, to the everyday opportunities of work and in our communities, Christians are faced with the challenge of a ministry of change. It is time to take on that challenge.

CHAPTER 9

Bringing About Change

A number of years ago, we bought a new home in a development where the builder had many houses in various stages of completion. He promised to have our house completed by an agreed-upon moving date. When we moved in almost all the work was done, and we were assured it would be completed shortly. Nothing happened.

Numerous calls to the builder simply generated excuses and more promises. He acknowledged that he had a moral and legal obligation, but he still failed to show up. I realized that people were lining up to buy his other new homes and, in order to close his sales with them, he had to keep his crews busy on these units. He had no self-interest to fulfill in completing our home other than to collect the escrow fund. He was willing to wait for that, because there was far more financial gain for him in completing the sales on additional units. I debated whether to get a lawyer involved, but that would cost me money. How could I touch his self-interest?

Many prospective buyers for his houses were driving past ours to get a feel for our development, and it occurred to me that a sign on our front lawn might do the trick. So I made a large sign saying, "I'm sorry I bought this house. Please ask me why." I placed it on a stake in our front lawn one Saturday morning. Only one prospective buyer stopped to inquire; but the builder's sales agent apparently saw the sign, because on Monday morning the workers were at our home to complete their unfinished tasks.

Clearly, my sign had threatened his primary interest of selling more homes. The only way to remove that threat was to do what he knew he was obligated to do anyway. The builder was not an evil man. He was very likable, and he did good work. By ignoring my pleas, he quite possibly might have been meeting the needs of several families. Perhaps he had some greater moral obligations to others than to me. But by tapping into his primary self-interest at that time, I was able to change his thinking and get him to do the right thing toward us. Was I wrong in targeting his self-interest? Should I have simply continued to appeal to his sense of morality? I might have had a very long wait.

SELF-INTEREST

Most of us operate out of self-interest most of the time. Life seldom presents us with clear and unambiguous choices. Various parties in a given situation will have differing interests to be met. The key to bringing about change is to find ways to satisfy the greatest amount of interest of all parties.

William Droel and Gregory Pierce point out that

> self-interest is the proper attention to one's own interests *in the context of the interests of others*. To pursue our self-interest is not to be selfish. Selfishness is the *exclusive* regard for ourselves, a point of view fixed solely on our own private advantage. Selfishness is clearly an evil and ultimately self-destructive. . . . Self-interest, however, makes people responsive to one another. It is the dynamic of society.[1]

Some purists argue that Christians should *always* put the welfare of others before their own interests. In a perfect world that philosophy would be ideal; but not everyone supports that principle. Therefore, in trying to bring about change, we need to consider the self-interest of those people and organizations we hope to change.

In a way self-interest is at the root of everything we do. Whenever I put the welfare of others before my own interests, am I not thereby satisfying a self-interest of wanting to be a moral person or to behave in a Christian manner? "Maybe by arguing self-interest," said Governor Mario Cuomo of New York, "we can teach the good uses of compassion."[2]

INDUCEMENTS FOR CHANGE

In *God's Agents for Change* I listed four types of inducements for change.[3] These inducements are orders, legislation, moral persuasion, and negotiation. Let's look at each one.

Orders

The first inducement comes as a result of an order by a person or persons in authority. For example, we use orders to change the behavior of our children when they do not honor a simple request. The CEO's order to the company to sell one of its divisions to another company also results in change. When the President of the United States issues an executive order, there is change. When the Supreme Court declares a law unconstitutional, there is change. When an OSHA inspector finds an unsafe working condition in a factory, there is change.

Society grants certain degrees of authority to many people to effect change in limited areas: teachers, police, air traffic controllers, athletic coaches, building inspectors, and employers are some examples. In recent years the absolute authority of persons in these positions has been limited somewhat by a greater attention to the rights of the individual. Nevertheless, the use of authority is still a very common way of bringing about change.

Legislation

The second inducement for change is connected with our process of enacting laws to bring it about. Pollution control laws have changed the environment in many parts of our nation. Laws governing the safety and fuel consumption of automobiles have changed the design and construction of the cars we drive. Occupational Safety and Health laws have changed working conditions in many industries. Although there is a commonly shared myth that "you can't legislate morality," the truth is that laws have changed the moral values we hold. Laws against child labor and slavery have shaped our morality on these issues. Laws against discrimination in employment, housing, and public accommodations are moving us toward a much more open society.

Of course, if laws are not obeyed, they fail to accomplish their purpose. Prohibition failed for this reason. And how many of us strictly obey the posted speed limits on our highways?

Nevertheless, legislation that is supported by a majority of the population will bring about change. For the change agent this may be a long and arduous means to bring about change, but in the long run it may be the only one to use.

Moral Persuasion

The third inducement for change is moral persuasion. A city council may decide to allocate funds for providing shelter to the homeless as a result of citizens who persuade council members that this is the "moral" thing to do. A company in a major city will "adopt" a local high school and provide resources to it to help raise the quality of education among the students. A convenience store near the junior high school will agree not to sell magazines and books which the PTA feels is offensive.

Moral persuasion is seldom an effective inducement for change unless there is an indirect benefit that will help the person or organization making the change. For example, the city council might provide funds for the homeless in the hope that it will help the retail stores in its downtown area. The company may adopt a high school in the hope that other companies will follow and, thereby, improve the education and skills of future employees. The convenience store may remove the offensive materials because it does not want the matter to escalate into a boycott of the entire store by members of the PTA.

Moral persuasion is the inducement for change most frequently promoted by religious organizations. It may make the churches feel virtuous, but, by itself, it seldom gets results.

Negotiation

The fourth inducement for change is the negotiating process, which takes into consideration the self-interests of various parties.

The sign that I put on the lawn was a part of my negotiations with the builder of my home to complete his work. The changes brought about by labor contracts result from a process in which the needs of both parties are negotiated to a point of mutual satisfaction. Neither side is completely satisfied, but both sides agree that it is a reasonable compromise of conflicting desires. The threat of legal action on charges of wrongful discharge is causing many companies to change the way they evaluate and document employee performance. Thus the mere threat of a possible confrontation with a disgruntled employee can cause a change in a company's practices.

A Combination of Inducements

Frequently, change comes about as a result of several of the four inducements coming into play at the same time. A story from Judy's experience is a good illustration.

Judy's relationship with Claire grew out of her prison ministry. It was through contacts with women such as Claire that Judy came to recognize that a larger issue needed to be addressed in our county: the terrible conditions of the prison itself.

Like many prisons in our country, the Lehigh County prison was old and overcrowded. The women's section was especially bad. There were only ten small cells to accommodate as many as twenty-seven women. Many slept on mattresses on the floor. The recreation area was simply a stairway landing. Each cell had an open toilet, and the flushing system for all the toilets was controlled by male guards in the central prison. Consequently, toilets were flushed only twice a day. On top of this there was no air-conditioning. Judy said that, on some hot summer days, the temperature soared to over 100 degrees Fahrenheit—so hot that it was impossible to grab the steel handrails. Unarguably, the prison was a hell hole.

Judy first appealed for help to the warden. He was sympathetic, but he had no authority to change the physical conditions. Her subsequent appeals to the county commissioners were virtually ignored.

Judy refused to give up. She began to get other people, mostly women, interested in the problem. Soon a coalition of twenty organizations formed in support of a new women's prison annex.

Representatives of the coalition met with the county commissioners, who politely listened to them but did nothing. Moral persuasion was getting nowhere.

Judy then made the decision to run for the elected office of county commissioner. The women's coalition supported her, but she was defeated. Two years later, however, she tried again. This time she won, becoming the first woman to be elected to that office.

Now she had some power and now people began to listen to her. She was no longer simply a "do-gooder housewife." She gained support for having outside prison experts come in to review the situation, and gradually won the support of a few of the male commissioners.

Judy now had the authority to introduce a bill calling for the construction of a new women's prison annex. With the support of some of her commissioner associates, and with the continued pressure from the coalition, it became apparent to the other commissioners that their own self-interest would be best served by voting for Judy's bill.

More than six years after she first became concerned about the problem, Judy attended the ground-breaking for a new women's prison annex. She had successfully combined several types of inducements for the county leaders to bring about change.

TACTICS FOR CHANGE

The above illustration prompts consideration of the tactics for change. There are a wide variety of tactics, some of which are more confrontational than others. We can group tactics into four categories: *education, appeals and petitions, moderate confrontation,* and *intense confrontation.*

Education

Education is the starting point for every change agent. People must first be made aware of the nature of the situation that calls for change. In some instances the public has already been well educated on the problem. When President Bush declared his war on drugs, for example, it was not necessary to give the American public a great deal of education about the nature of the drug problem; they already knew. In other instances, however, the public may know little or nothing. Do you know the specific *degree* of the drug problem in your community? Or AIDS? Or homelessness? Or discrimination in housing? Before any movement for change on these issues can happen in your community, people will have to be educated.

Education can take place through public meetings, press conferences, circulating leaflets, writing letters to newspapers, and getting on radio talk shows. It has been my experience that the public response to open educational meetings is directly proportional to their self-interest. Hold an open meeting on fair housing, and you will attract only those who are already concerned and those who have experienced discrimination. Hold an open meeting on redistricting the school system, however, and you will get crowds of people.

Change seldom occurs through education alone, but it is an absolute prerequisite for any other types of tactics.

Appeals and Petitions

The next level of tactics, *appeals and petitions*, involves contacts made directly with the authorities who are in a position to bring about change. Letters, personal visits, phone calls, petitions, paid advertisements in the newspaper, and shareholder resolutions are good examples. These were the tactics Terry Rakolta used in dealing with the companies that sponsored what she felt were offensive television programs.

Opinions vary about the effectiveness of sending letters to one's representative in congress. Although few letters get beyond the staff, attention is given to the *number* of letters that arrive on a specific issue—especially if they are original in composition. Some legislators are turned off by mass mailings of identical letters or postcards that have been orchestrated by a special interest group.

By chance, however, I have discovered how to ensure that my US representative in Washington will read my letters. One day I happened to be seated two rows behind him on a morning flight to Washington, DC. I saw that as soon as he sat down, he took the local newspaper out of his briefcase and turned immediately to the editorial page. The very first thing he read were the letters to the editor. Since then I have observed that whenever I or one of my friends gets a letter to the editor published that mentions our representative in some way, a reply is forthcoming, either personally or in the letters to the editor column.

A personal visit to the mayor or corporate president or US Senator is highly desirable; but staffs are very protective and personal visits may be difficult to arrange. One way to get a hearing with a busy public official is to secure a large list of names on a petition dealing with your concern. Since you are representing the people who signed the petition, there is a much better chance that you will be given time to present your case.

Earlier we discussed shareholder resolutions. Not too many people are aware of this potential avenue of presenting a concern to a corporation whose stock is publicly traded. The Securities and Exchange Commission, which oversees matters related to corporate stocks, has provided that any shareholder who owns at least $2,000 worth of stock, or one hundred shares for at least one year, can file a shareholder resolution with his or her company. This resolution must be presented at the annual shareholders' meeting and be voted upon by all holders of stock in that company. The rules prohibit filing frivolous or vindictive resolutions, or ones that deal with ordinary business matters. But matters that can affect the future of the company are generally permitted.

The filing of shareholder resolutions has been primarily an activity of large pension funds, especially those of churches. In recent years the pension funds of public employees and college teachers have also become very active. The biggest issue for the past ten years has dealt with the activities of American companies having operations in South Africa. Shareholder resolutions also appear every year on such issues as environmental pollution, equal employment, marketing of harmful products, infant formula marketing, production of nuclear materials, and corporate governance.

Shareholders who write letters to their corporate leaders invariably get responses. If the responses are not satisfactory, filing a shareholder resolution frequently prompts an invitation for a consultation. CEOs do not like to have their annual meetings cluttered up with shareholder resolutions, even though they usually get a very low percentage of votes. If the shareholder's request is reasonable, the company may offer to negotiate an action that will meet the needs of the shareholder; in this case the shareholder agrees to withdraw the resolution. If there is no consultation or if a consultation does not yield satisfactory results, the resolution must be presented at the annual shareholders' meeting, and must appear on the proxy ballot. At the meeting the proposer of the resolution and other supporters of it have the right to address the entire board of directors on the issue of concern. All the proxy votes are counted and reported at the meeting. If a sufficient percentage of votes is received, the same resolution can be resubmitted the following year.[4]

Moderate and Intense Confrontation

The third and fourth levels of tactics are *confrontational*. To "confront" means to come in front of, to oppose. The tactics of education and appeals and petitions are in the nature of requesting the other side to come along with you. In confrontation, however, sides have been drawn and pressure is applied to make some person or some organization do that which they want not to do.

You can choose from a wide variety of confrontational tactics. In a moderate form of confrontation, you apply pressure but give the other party the option to change or not to change. In the intense form of confrontation, you make the effort to force the other party to comply because all other tactics have failed. The terms moderate and intense do not relate to levels of force or violence, since violence can occur with either tactic.

Labor negotiations are examples of *moderate confrontation*. Both sides make demands upon the other, but each side has the option to agree or not agree. When agreement cannot be reached, the tactics escalate to a level of high confrontation, with either the union going on strike or management locking out the workers. Each side tries to force the other to change.

When I placed the sign on my lawn, I engaged the builder in a form of moderate confrontation. He could have ignored my sign and continued to let me wait. Had I gone to court and secured a judgment against him, it would have been intense confrontation, for he would have been forced to do what I wanted.

The so-called Gandhi style of peaceful protest is an example of moderate confrontation. It was the style of much of the civil rights movement in the 1960s. When blacks boarded interstate buses and sat at segregated lunch counters awaiting service that never came, they were engaged in moderate confrontation. The law was on their side; they were simply giving the white folks the opportunity to obey the law voluntarily. In this case moderate confrontation sometimes evoked violent reaction on the part of the whites, and many blacks were beaten and murdered. When court orders were issued and federal marshalls began riding the busses, the level of confrontation became intense. The whites had to obey or they went to jail.

Sometimes people use dramatic confrontational tactics to arouse more support for a cause. When antiwar protesters invaded the General Electric Space Center to pour blood over missiles, their primary objective was to gain greater support for their cause. When antinuclear demonstraters blocked the entrances to nuclear test sites or missile sites with their bodies, their primary hope was that their actions would evoke a nationwide support for their cause. Sometimes the media label such demonstrations "symbolic." Maybe so. But for those who may be beaten and hauled off to jail it is quite real.

Most people dislike confrontation, and for good reason. It is not pleasant, and usually it is not popular. I recall how dramatically my moods shifted during the Vietnam War protests. When I was among thousands marching for a cause, the group euphoria reinforced my conviction that the cause was just. But the next day, when I sat in the corporate manager's dining room and my friends and associates made it clear that they disagreed intensely with my viewpoint and my tactics, I found that the ministry of change could be a very lonely one.

Sometimes the ministry of change causes us to confront the people or organizations we love. That is difficult and painful.

When I took early retirement from Bethlehem Steel Corporation in 1981 to do consulting for organizations engaged in both profit and nonprofit activities, I knew my level of income would drop significantly. But one of the factors that helped me to decide was the knowledge that, in retirement, the company would continue to cover health insurance for me and my family, and that a company-paid life insurance policy would be maintained with my wife as beneficiary. That pledge was in writing in my booklet of benefits for retirees.

A year after I retired, the steel industry went into a tailspin and experienced one of the worst recessions it has ever known. Thousands of workers were laid off and many facilities were closed. As part of Bethlehem Steel's cost-cutting program, management announced that it was going to change the health benefits for retirees. That caused me great concern—not so much about the nature of the change, but about the precedent it would set. If the company could change any part of its promises to retirees, they could change it all, including the complete abolition of health benefits and insurance coverage. That would be bad news for me and disastrous for retirees with low pension payments.

I wrote to the chairman of the company, whom I had known on a personal basis, pointing out that the company could not revoke its pledges to retirees. His reply explained why this had to be done for practical reasons, but the message was clear: The company felt it had the right to do as it wished with its promises to retirees. I appealed in another letter, indicating that I was prepared to seek legal counsel unless the decision was reversed. His reply was unchanged.

I started legal proceedings that ultimately involved a class action suit against Bethlehem Steel on behalf of 18,000 retirees. We held meetings, secured $25 donations from other retirees, and raised enough funds to cover some of the legal expenses. I was not surprised that the management I used to work with quite amicably a few years earlier had no kind words or thoughts for what I was doing. Occasionally, a former associate would tell me privately that he supported our cause, but in the eyes of the company I was a pariah. In the eyes of the retirees, on the other hand, I was their champion.

Perhaps the most uncomfortable moments came in the federal courtroom in Buffalo, New York, where the trial was being held. I was one of many called to the witness stand. After my testimony I was cross-examined by a Bethlehem Steel attorney with whom I used to work closely when I was still manager of sales. In that courtroom former friends had become intense adversaries.

We won the lawsuit, and the company moved to appeal. The day before the case was to go to the appellate court in New York

City, the company offered a settlement in which they guaranteed never to take away our promised benefits. In exchange we would participate to some extent in sharing the cost of health benefits. We agreed to do so because the company was in serious financial trouble. Some of the pensioners wanted it all, but I and the other leaders of the class action suit felt the settlement was fair. Today the company is doing well, but I still feel some resentment from some of my former associates as a result of what I did.

THE NEED FOR SUPPORT GROUPS

The ministry of change can be a hard one if it requires intensive levels of confrontation. Because of this it is very important for people engaged in change to have a support group. Christian support groups are needed for effective ministry in all the styles described in this book, but they are especially important when we are engaged in a ministry of change.

A Christian support group is a cluster of people who meet on a regular basis over an extended period of time in order to share with each other the struggles—and joys—of relating faith to daily life. My Monday Connection group is one example of a Christian support group, but there are many others.

Support groups can meet on a weekly, biweekly, or monthly basis. When a group stays together over a long period of time, the members come to know and care for each other very deeply. As a member of such a group, you can discuss very frankly issues that concern you, with the expectation that other members of the group will listen carefully, offer suggestions, raise questions, and express support.

Support groups can be structured in a variety of ways. During the years that Judy was working to bring about change in the women's prison, she received immense support from members of her coalition, who met regularly. It was they who encouraged her to run for public office, and they worked to see that she was ultimately elected. To this day Judy maintains strong ties with members of that coalition.

In the class action suit begun against Bethlehem Steel, my support group was issue oriented and consisted of other members of the retirees who formed our steering committee. We shared our concerns and doubts and supported each other in our efforts to bring about change.

Support groups can also be formed in the workplace. In many offices and factories, small clusters of Christians gather on a regular basis for Bible study, prayer, or discussion.

I have found it important to be in a congregational support group in addition to other issue-oriented groups, such as those described above. In the past Judy and I have been members of an ecumenical support group, and children were included in many of our gatherings. Currently, we are members of a *koinonia* group, consisting of eleven couples, all of whom are members of our congregation. Twenty-two members is a bit on the large size, but many of us travel and the group rarely meets in its entirety. We meet on the second Sunday evening of each month in the home of one the members. The host family usually serves dessert and coffee, which provides time for socializing. Next, the host family offers a brief devotional reading and the group joins in prayer. Then we get into our topic for the evening. Frequently, we do joint study of books with a religious theme. However, if someone has a personal problem or concern they wish to share with the rest of the group, we put the discussion topic to one side in order to deal with the concern being raised. We stop promptly at 10:00 P.M. with the singing of a hymn.

The congregational support group provides the opportunity for suggestions and feedback from close friends who are not directly involved in your ministry of change. When you get caught up in a cause, it is possible to get carried away and lose touch with the viewpoints of people who are not involved in your efforts. When we spend time exclusively with like-minded people in a particular cause, it is easy to overlook some factors people who are not involved can see. Furthermore, a good support group can gently help you see where you may be making a mistake.

The ministry of change is important for many Christians, but it can be lonely and confusing as we work within the highly complex structures of our society. At times it requires great courage. God will nourish us in our ministry of change. We make God's job easier if the channels are open for God to reach us through an association of loving and supporting Christian believers.

VI

LIFE-STYLE

CHAPTER 10

The Need to Give

Once each day some customer at the Hausman's Precision Welding shop gets a big surprise: There is no charge for the work. No one— not even the owners, Ron and Judy Hausman—knows at the beginning of a day who it will be. "It just happens," says Ron. "At some point in the day I get the feeling that the next one to come in the door is for free."

I had known Ron and Judy for perhaps ten years before this little secret of theirs came out. They have always been very generous givers, both to our congregation and especially when they hear of a person or family with a special need. When I learned of their practice of giving someone a no-charge billing once each day, I wanted to know why.

"God has given us so much in our lives," explained Ron, "much more than we ever expected. Every day he sends us blessings. And it's all free, with no merit of our own. So we just decided that we'd do the same thing with at least one of our customers each day."

"How do you decide?" I asked.

"There's no plan," he explained. "We don't try to select the most needy person, or the best customer, or the most friendly one. There just comes a time each day when Judy or I feel the urge to not charge for our work. So, we don't. That's all."

"I'll bet people are surprised," I said.

"Yeah, it's funny sometimes. They can't believe it. Many of them think there's a catch to it. Some of them insist on paying, but we refuse to take the money."

"What do you tell them?"

"I just say that it's a gift from us. I tell them that God has given us so many gifts that we want to give a gift to them." He paused. "I really don't know if it is God's urging that makes us give to a certain person. I just know that we feel we need to share a part of what we have received."

"You know, it's funny," he said. "Most people don't know how to receive a free gift. One lady resisted so much that she came back the next day with a big cake she baked for us. She just couldn't accept our free gift. I think a lot of us are that way about God. We can't believe that the gifts we have been given have been without merit."

Ron and Judy Hausman have never studied theology, but they are topnotch theologians.

It's not as if they are making tons of money. They aren't. They have a good welding business that provides them with a comfortable income. They don't live pretentiously. Although Judy has had some serious health problems, they are always very positive about their lives. But the driving force in their lives is a deep gratitude for all the blessings they have received, and a strong conviction that they want to share as much as they can with others.

The Hausmans have a ministry of life-style. It is so different from what our society considers normal that it causes people to think and, possibly, to copy.

Compare Ron and Judy Hausman with the college student in my class in "Religion, Ethics and Business" who, upon hearing a number of my comments about Wall Street greed, asked in all seriousness: "What's wrong with greed?"

How would you answer that question? In a recent visit with a well-known Christian author, I asked how he would have responded to the student. He said that he would point out that we live in a world where some have much and some have little and that we need to share with others. That answer might have worked with college students twenty years ago, but it doesn't wash today. For many young people today the driving concern is, "What's in this for me?" In fact, until the high flying Wall Street trader, Ivan Boesky, ended up in prison, his strong defense of greed was a popular topic in many social gatherings.

My answer to the student was that I have never met or known of a greedy person who was truly happy. Greed, by its very nature, is always seeking more. There is never enough. The greedy person is never satisfied, never fulfilled, never happy. That response touched the student's individualistic orientation.

Not all students are so egocentric, and it is good to know that times apparently are changing. I am beginning to encounter more students who have a broader view of life. Meanwhile, however, almost an entire generation has been nurtured on a diet of materialism, status, power, and self-gratification. The effect of this generation of Americans on our society as a whole has been devastating. We are cynical. We don't trust anybody or any institution.

In *The Cynical Americans: Living and Working in an Age of Discontent,* Donald Kanter and Phillip Mirvis paint a disturbing picture of how Americans have come to mistrust people in general and institutions in particular.[1] Their broad study revealed that in the late 1950s more than 80 percent of Americans trusted government, yet barely one in four do so today. Twenty years ago public trust in business and its leaders stood at 70 percent; today it is only 15 percent. Sixty percent of Americans today believe that most people will lie if they can gain from it; and 72 percent believe there is a growing loss of basic trust and faith in other people. Cynicism is highest among those age twenty-four and younger and least among those over thirty-five. Where is the idealism of youth? Even among older people cynicism is growing, to the point that in November 1988 the American Association of Retired Persons spent $400,000 in an effort to get cynical retirees to vote.

Kanter and Mirvis feel that the greed and dishonesty of the 1980s bodes poorly for the outlook of the next generation. "There has been an institutionalization of greed in this country, where everybody thinks it's a birthright to get his. The answer is not everybody is going to get it. Not everybody can climb the slippery slope. Under the circumstances, we think it is going to make for a lot more disillusionment, which leads to cynicism."[2]

Public cynicism is not new. It is healthy to maintain a bit of cynicism, because it presses one toward the truth. But the kind of deep, pervasive cynicism in which employees don't trust their bosses, voters don't trust their elected officials, college students are out for the big buck, slick entrepreneurs are ruthless toward others, and people cease to be civil with each other, is going to destroy the fabric of our society unless it is reversed.

The historian, Arthur Schlesinger, Jr., believes we are starting to move into a period when the pursuit of personal wealth will shift

to a pursuit of the commonwealth. He sees American society os-
cillating in thirty-year cycles between periods when private pur-
suits and self-indulgence prevail (the Roaring Twenties, the
Eisenhower Years, the Money Society of the 1980s) and periods
where social activism and common purpose predominate (the Progressive Era at the beginning of this century, the New Deal, the
New Frontier of the early 1960s). Schlesinger has great expectations
for those older "baby boomers" born between 1946 and 1957. He
predicts that as they rise to positions of leadership, they will bring
with them the heady idealism they soaked up during the 1960s.[3]

While some critics may feel that Schlesinger is romanticizing
the 1960s, the first signs of a new concern for the common good are
beginning to appear. In his inaugural address George Bush said,
"We are not the sum of our possessions. We cannot hope only to
leave our children a bigger car, a bigger bank account. We must
hope to give them a sense of what it means to be a loyal friend: a
loving parent; a citizen who leaves his home, his neighborhood and
town better than he found it."[4]

Many Christians have been active participants in the decade of
conspicuous consumption, self-gratification, and the glorification
of unrestrained individualism. Of even greater shame than the rise
and fall of such profligate televangelists as Jim and Tammy Bakker
is the fact that millions of Christians approved and supported their
extravagant personal life-styles.

Christians need to take a hard and honest look at their personal
life-styles. We need to confess that we have been seduced by the
glitter of material goods and the glory of status. We need to bring
to our society a life-style of Jesus that values people above property,
caring above careerism, selflessness above self, and giving above
getting.

GIVING

You can begin to examine your life-style by taking into account
your giving patterns. Americans have, from their earliest days as a
nation, been noted for the degree to which they contribute their
money and their time for the welfare of others. The French historian, Alexis de Tocqueville, considered this trait to be one of the
most distinctive of the budding young nation. In recent years this

tradition of voluntary giving has been pressed in the political bat-
tlefields by those who argue that big government is not the best
channel for meeting the needs of society. Ronald Reagan's call for
greater volunteerism and George Bush's "thousand points of light"
are examples of this philosophy. So how are we doing as a nation?

A 1988 Gallup study, commissioned by Independent Sector, revealed that 71 percent of all those surveyed indicated that their
household contributed to charity. The average of all contributions
was $790 per year or 1.9 percent of household income. About 9 per-
cent of the respondents reported that their households contributed
5 percent or more to charity. With respect to the volunteering of
time, 45 percent of the respondents indicated they contributed an
average of 4.7 hours per week to charity.[5]

By a wide margin the greatest benefactors of voluntary giving
are religious organizations. Of those households which reported
giving, 52.5 percent contributed to religious organizations for an average of $715 per year. Approximately 70 percent of all individual
charitable contributions go to churches and religious organizations.
The next highest category of giving was to health organizations (including hospitals) with 24 percent of contributing households giving an average of $130 per year. Another 24 percent contributed an
average of $210 per year to human services agencies. While edu-
cational institutions received gifts from only 15 percent of giving
households, the average was $293 per year. The arts, culture, and
humanities received an average gift of $260 per year, but from only
8 percent of those households that give. Other beneficiaries listed
in the report are youth development organizations; environment,
international, private, and community foundations; and public and
societal benefit organizations.

As a percentage of income, those households with incomes less
than $10,000 per year gave more than any other income grouping.
They were well above average in their giving to religious organizations, and somewhat below average in giving to other charities.
As a percentage of income, families with three or more children
gave more than those with one or two children. Widows were the
type of family unit which gave the highest percent of income, average 3.4 percent.[6]

The studies focused on the giving behavior of Americans and
explored their motives for giving. It was clear from all the studies
that Americans believe individuals should contribute to charities.

While there did not seem to be a clear relationship between religious giving and giving to other charities, those individuals who gave to both were much higher in their contributions to nonreligious charities than those who gave only to other charities. We will look at this finding again later.

There is a strong relationship between those who volunteer their time and those who make financial contributions. As household income increases, so does the proportion of low-level givers. With respect to motives, the researchers found that a strong commitment to certain personal goals and values had a marked impact on the level of household giving and on volunteering.

The researchers came to a firm conclusion that Americans have a capacity for increased giving of both time and money. Thirty-eight percent of the people surveyed expressed the belief that they should be giving more. This finding has led Independent Sector to propose that by 1991 the contributions of Americans could be averaging 5 percent of their income and five hours a week of their time.[7]

It is quite clear from all of the above that religious institutions have been effective in developing giving habits among their members. And for good reason. It is obvious from a reading of the Bible that the people of God are called to give, as a response to all that they have received. Very early in the Old Testament, we encounter the admonition that the firstborn of the cattle and sheep and crops are to be offered to God (Exodus 22:30; 23:19). "All the tithe of the land, whether of the seed of the land or the fruit of the trees, is the Lord's: it is holy to the Lord" (Leviticus 27:30 RSV). The same principles of proportionate giving and first-fruits giving were urged upon the early Christian church by the Apostle Paul. To the church at Corinth he wrote, "On the first day of every week, each of you is to put something aside and store it up, as he may prosper, so that contributions need not be made when I come" (1 Corinthians 16:2 NIV).

Jesus commended the poor widow for giving so generously out of her poverty; and in his parable of Lazarus, he condemned those who overlooked the needy. He warned about storing up one's riches here on earth, "where moths and rust destroy, and robbers break in and steal." Jesus scoffed at the greed that would cause an already wealthy farmer to tear down his barns to make room for bigger ones to store his goods. He warned his followers to, "Watch out and guard yourselves from every kind of greed; because a person's true life is not made up of the things he owns, no matter how rich he may be." When he sent out his disciples to minister in his name, he told them, "You have received without paying, so give without being paid" (Luke 16:19–31; Matthew 6:19 TEV; Luke 12:16–21; Luke 12:15 TEV; Matthew 10:8b TEV).

Although the Old Testament admonitions and the teachings of Jesus clearly raise a concern for the poor, there is a second, equally important, reason why we should give: It is the need of the giver to give. Giving is the only way we can ensure against the greed that places possessions above God. Giving is the only way we can express gratitude for what we have received. Giving is another of the ways we experience spirituality.

In all my life I have never met a generous person who was not happy. It is as much a certainty for me as is the law of gravity.

If Christians take seriously the need of the giver to give, a powerful ministry of values can be delivered to a society sickened by greed. The studies on giving in America have demonstrated that the churches have had great success in motivating people to give to their religious institutions. It remains for the churches to widen the scope of giving to include the whole of creation instead of only religious institutions.

REAL STEWARDSHIP

It is unfortunate that most of our churches have severely narrowed the biblical understanding of stewardship. A steward is defined in the dictionary as "a person who manages another's property or financial affairs, or who administers anything as the agent of another."[8] That is precisely the way the word is used in the Bible: The steward in the Old Testament and in the parables of Jesus was always one who was called upon to manage the affairs or property of another. The Christian principle of stewardship says that since we brought nothing into this world and can take nothing with us when we die, everything we have really belongs to God; we are entrusted with these possessions to use as God's agents. We are accountable to God for everything.

Unfortunately, most religious organizations, in their efforts to raise money, have narrowed the understanding of stewardship exclusively to mean that one gives to the church a part of what one has earned. That concept is faulty on two counts: First, it implies that our possessions are truly *ours*, not that which we hold in trust for our God. Second, it suggests that the only response a Christian can make out of gratitude is to give something to the church.

We need to get straight in our minds that *everything* we have is really held in trust for God, and we are to use *everything* as responsible stewards. God is concerned for what we give away and what we keep for our own use. In this chapter the focus is on that which we give away; in the next chapter we will deal with that which we retain for our own use.

If we take seriously what the Bible has to say about stewardship and giving, the model for the contemporary Christian is this: We establish a commitment to lay aside on each payday ("first-fruits") a certain percentage of income ("freely have you received; freely give") to be used as we feel God would wish (stewardship) on behalf of God's whole creation ("for the whole world is mine").

When Judy and I were first challenged with this concept of stewardship by two laymembers of our little church in Detroit, it was scary. When they suggested that a tithe of everything I brought home on payday should be a minimum level for giving, it seemed absolutely impossible. When they indicated that our tithe would be used not just for our own congregation, but wherever we felt called to give in the name of Jesus Christ, it seemed almost heretical. But they showed me a way to start. I followed their suggestion that, starting with my level of less than 2 percent, each time I received a raise from my employer I would add 1 percent to my proportionate giving. In about five years we were at the 10 percent level and it fit into our budgets very comfortably. We later moved from 10 percent of net income to 10 percent of gross income. As we reached the period in life when we could invest money in various financial instruments, we included investment income for tithing.

The most meaningful part of our stewardship program was deciding how we should use the money we laid aside each payday. We said it was dedicated for God's purposes. In fact, we called the little box in which we kept the money our "Lord's Treasury." The largest single part of that fund went to our local church; but we decided as a family how the rest could be best used. Some money went to help people whom we knew were in need. One of our daughters got interested in sponsoring an orphan child in Asia, and some money went there. We helped to sponsor refugees from Germany, Cuba, Uganda, and Vietnam. We sent some money for hunger appeals. When the doorbell rang and someone asked for money, we never felt pressured to give, for money was at hand. Rather, we judged whether giving to the cause was the best stewardship of what we had put aside for giving. It was easy to say no if the cause was not the best.

The giving program we were introduced to some thirty years ago has profoundly affected our lives. At times we have to explain to our pastors why, when we do have money put aside for giving, it does not all go to our congregation. Church leaders often assume that when Christians tithe, it all goes to the church. Yet we know from experience that if a congregation can get a substantial number of its members on the Lord's Treasury program, they can give to a variety of causes and there will still always be enough money to meet the needs of the church.

STEWARDSHIP OF TIME

In the same way that we are called to be stewards of the material possessions God has entrusted to us, we are also to be good stewards of the time we have been given. From time to time I hear or read admonitions from well-meaning Christians about the use of their time. The presentations follow the same pattern: Start with the 168 hours of the week and deduct from it 56 hours of sleep, 50 hours connected with work, 17 hours given to eating, and so on, until there remains only 1 to 3 hours a week devoted to attending church and praying at home. We are then made to feel guilty that only 1.5 percent of our time goes to God. The message is unmistakable: God's only concern for our time is when we are doing "religious" things. But isn't God concerned about how we use *all* of those 168 hours? Isn't he concerned that we get enough sleep and food to stay healthy, and do enough work to keep ourselves and our families clothed, fed, and sheltered?

The church has a way of making us feel guilty when we aren't involved in church-related activities. The commonly understood definition of a "dedicated layperson" is someone who sings on the choir, assists in the worship service, teaches in the church school, serves on three committees, attends district church conventions, and sets up chairs for the congregational dinners. It is never the one who drives for Meals on Wheels, or provides shelter for a foreign student, or sorts garments at the center city clothing bank, or serves as a nurse's aid at a nursing home, or teaches a young man in prison to read. Yet if we take Jesus' words seriously, that is exactly what a dedicated layperson should be doing (Matthew 25:31–46).

The fact is that the way in which we use our 168 hours per week is a measurement of our stewardship for God. To each of us is given the same number of hours each week. We can waste those hours, but we cannot make more of them. It is imperative that we allocate enough time to carry out our ministries in the family, the workplace, the community, and the church. There are hundreds of causes to which we could give our time, so we must be selective. Many a committed Christian has become so involved in a badly needed community project that the ministry to family has suffered. Many a social worker or clergy person has become so overcommitted to the needs of the job that they suffer burnout.

The stewardship of my money is one way I can support a cause while limiting my commitment of time to it. I don't have the time or the talent to be working with prisoners in our local county jail, although I do believe in the importance of rehabilitation. So we send money to Grace Episcopal Church, which is a block away from the prison and runs a prison ministry program there, and to the Program for Female Offenders.

Independent Sector calls for Americans to be "fivers"—to give 5 percent of their income to charity and to contribute five hours a week in volunteerism.[9] Isn't this the time for Christians to raise the ante? Since the principle of the tithe has strong biblical roots, and since there needs to be a bold statement against the acceptance of greed, the time is ripe for millions of Christians to follow the principle of the tithe. It would be a glorious statement of values, and would be of immeasurable help to thousands of social service agencies, community organizations and churches that are struggling to keep alive.

Should we then also double the ante for giving five hours a week in volunteerism? This may pose a problem for many people, except possibly for those who are retired and have fulfilled most of their family responsibilities. For those who are working, are parents, and are trying to keep their sanity in a world that is increasingly hectic, five hours a week of volunteerism outside the home, including church volunteer work, may be as much as one can handle responsibly. Volunteerism outside the home should not be given higher importance than our ministries within the home, particularly when we have children. So perhaps Christians can talk about being "ten-fivers": 10 percent of income for giving and five hours a week given in volunteer work outside the home.

Ten-fivers! What a powerful statement it would be if every member of every church in America became a ten-fiver. Even if half of them would. Even one-third? Yes, even if it is just you and I, we can make a statement about our ministry of values.

CHAPTER 11

Living on the Low Side

One hot summer day, Bob Rodale, owner of Rodale Press, stopped by for a brief visit. He had been out walking, saw Judy drive by, and decided to visit us.

Judy and I have known Bob Rodale ever since high school. When we moved back to Allentown after twenty years of district sales office assignments with Bethlehem Steel, we built a home about a quarter-mile away from where Bob and Ardie had settled shortly after he completed college. Their home is a very modest one on what used to be the Rodale family compound. Bob's father, Jerry, launched Rodale Press into the big time with two magazines, *Prevention* and *Organic Gardening*. When Jerry Rodale died, Bob took over the reins of the company. Under his leadership it has become known throughout the world, as has Bob. Today the Rodale empire includes large experimental farms, and a modern printing plant that produces books and magazines on health habits, foods, exercise, farming, regeneration of the land, and a broad range of similar topics. The Rodale experimental farm and the old homestead have become almost shrines for visitors around the world who are interested in environmental issues. I frequently run into Bob at our airport as he departs for places like China, Africa, India, and Egypt. He frequently is asked to appear before congressional committees or to speak at international conferences.

With all the wealth that Rodale Press has brought in, and with all the worldwide recognition Bob has attained, he is still the modest, quiet person we knew back in high school. He watches his diet, almost to the point of appearing frail, yet it is clear that regular exercise keeps him fit. The Rodales own two cars, but they are far from the luxury models that other executives in our town drive. They are simple, rather nondescript cars, which have been around for quite a few years. Bob sometimes bikes the five miles to and from his office and sometimes walks.

On that hot day when Bob visited us, we offered him a drink. Of the list of possibilities, he selected a cold herbal tea that is popular in our family. As I looked at him, with his graying beard a bit wet from his walk in the hot sun, I could not help but think how atypical Bob Rodale is as a chief executive officer of a rather large company. He always dresses neatly, but simply and comfortably. One would never single him out in a crowded airplane as a well-known CEO, based on the way he was dressed.

Bob and Ardie Rodale have a very simple material life-style. Their home, their cars, their manner of dress, their eating and exercise habits all speak of simplicity. Well, you might say, if they want to promote books and magazines in the field of health and environmental issues, they had better live that kind of life. Otherwise they will be seen as hypocrites and phonies. What else should you expect from a family that is in the business they are in?*

That is precisely the point. Our life-style has much, if not everything, to say about the sincerity of our beliefs and commitments. I know the Rodales well enough to say that their life-style is not a sham just to enhance their business. Their life-style is an honest expression of their deep commitment to a philosophy of caring for the earth and its resources, and caring for the wellness and wholeness of humans everywhere.

Contrast Bob and Ardie Rodale with Jim and Tammy Bakker, whose commitment was claimed to be the spreading of the gospel of Jesus Christ. Their life-style of extravagant living from the very start of their ministry was a betrayal of the one whose message they sought to deliver.

---

*During the production of this book, Robert Rodale was tragically killed in an automobile accident in Moscow while working with Soviet officials on an agriculture project.

Shortly before his crucifixion, Jesus prayed on behalf of his followers:

> "I gave them your message, and the world hated them, because they do not belong to the world, just as I do not belong to the world. I do not ask you to take them out of the world, but I do ask you to keep them safe from the Evil One. Just as I do not belong to the world, they do not belong to the world. . . . I sent them into the world just as you sent me into the world." (John 17:14–17 TEV)

The world and the "Evil One" to which Jesus refers here are those things that divert one's worship away from God to other, smaller gods.

WORLDLY GODS

What are these worldly gods? Jesus named them many times in his ministry of preaching. They are "the worries about this life, the love for riches and all other kinds of desires." They are the treasures we store up for ourselves on earth and the worries of our lives, such as what we eat or drink or the clothes we wear. Jesus scorned those who, in order to gain the honor of others, give to the needy by announcing it with trumpets in the synagogues and on the streets, or pray standing in the synagogues and on the street corners to be seen by men (Mark 4:19 TEV; Matthew 6:19, 6:25, 6:2, 6:5). The worldly gods are those things which relate to ourselves rather than to God. And, of course, sin is putting oneself ahead of God.

Martin Luther wrote, "A god is that to which we look for all good and in which we find refuge in every time of need."[1] If our ultimate trust is in wealth, in possessions, in having power or status in life, in appearing to be honorable or noble in the sight of others, or in securing fame through some personal achievement, then we have been made captives of the world. We are owned by the world; we belong to the world. Jesus' final prayer for his followers was that they belong to God and not to the world. We, as Christians, are to be in the world but not of the world.

GOD PROVIDES ENOUGH

The Bible is very clear about the evil of exploiting the poor or powerless in order to gain more for oneself. "Shame on the man who builds his house by unjust means and completes its roof chambers by fraud, making his countrymen work without payment, giving them no wage for their labor" (Jeremiah 22:13 NEB). "The Lord enters into judgment against the elders and the leaders of his people: 'It is you who have ruined my vineyard; the plunder from the poor is in your houses. What do you mean by crushing my people and grinding the faces of the poor?' declares the Lord, the Lord Almighty" (Isaiah 3:14–15 NIV). And in Job 22:5–9 NIV:

> "Is not your wickedness great? Are not your sins endless? You demanded security from your brothers for no reason; you stripped men of their clothing, leaving them naked. You gave no water to the weary and you withheld food from the hungry, though you were a powerful man, owning land—an honored man, living on it. And you sent widows away empty-handed and broke the strength of the fatherless."

Amassing wealth or power for oneself at the expense of others is absolutely contrary to the will of God.

But another strain runs through the Bible. It deals with amassing for ourselves more than we need, even if it is *not* at the expense of others. Some have called it a "theology of enough." It goes this way: God provides for all creatures. If we trust God, then we need not take more from creation than we really need.

That principle first appears in Exodus 16, where we read the account of the Israelites in the desert following their flight from captivity in Egypt. In response to the need for food, God provided quail for the people to eat in the evening and manna each morning. Each person was instructed to take only as much as was needed for that day. Moses instructed them, "No one is to keep any of it until morning." Some, however, did not trust God to provide for the next day. "However, some of them paid no attention to Moses; they kept part of it until morning, but it was full of maggots and began to smell" (Exodus 16:20 NIV). Or, as the King James version says, "It bred worms and stank." On the day preceding a Sabbath, the people were instructed to take an extra day's ration so that they need not work on the holy day. On these days, however, the food did not spoil.

The point was to demonstrate that God would provide enough for the people, but they had to have trust. If we keep more than enough for ourselves, out of a distrust of God, we find that what we have saved ultimately "stinks."

Jesus repeats this theme when he speaks to his followers: "Do not store up for yourselves treasures on earth, where moth and rust destroy, and where thieves break in and steal. . . . For where your treasure is, there your heart will also be" (Matthew 6:19, 21 NIV).

If the promise to all God's children is that if they only trust they will receive enough to sustain life, why is it that there are so many poor and starving people in the world? Why does God permit people to starve to death? I do not know for certain the answer to that question, any more than I know why six million Jews were permitted to die in the Holocaust. But I do know that it was people—mostly Christian people, not God—who killed those Jews. Similarly, I know that there is enough extra money and food in some nations, mostly Christian nations, to keep most of the people on this earth, perhaps all of them, from starving. Yes, I know all the complex problems connected with the distribution of food and resources from the "haves" to the "have-nots" in this world, and I plead guilty to throwing up my hands in despair when trying to find a way to solve those problems. But that is not to say that God has not provided the resources. God has. The problem is that God's children have found neither the will nor the way to get them distributed equitably.

Much has been written and spoken about the uneven distribution of other resources in the world. The wealthy one-third of the nations account for 87 percent of the world's gross national product. That means that the poor two-thirds get only 13 percent! The United States alone, with only 5 percent of the world's population, currently consumes 44 percent of the world's coal, 42 percent of its aluminum, 38 percent of its nickel, and earns 40 percent of the world's income![2]

Not only do we need to concern ourselves with the maldistribution of the earth's resources, we must also face up to the fact that the earth is a finite planet. It truly is a spaceship. There is an absolute limit to the oil, coal, and minerals it will yield. Even resources that seem to be inexhaustible, such as air, water, and light, can be so abused as to render this planet uninhabitable for some future generation. All this has been said so many times before that it seems to be of little consequence to many of us. But it is true: We can make this planet incapable of sustaining human life, and it need not take a nuclear war to do it.

Clearly, there is ample reason for all the world's people to practice a theology of enough. There is a *compelling* reason for Christians to do so: God's will is that we do so.

The ministry of life-style does not stand apart from the ministries of competency, presence, ethics, and change. It is integrated into them. That means that our life-style should be just enough to accomplish the other ministries effectively.

MARION SANDLER

The relationship between life-style and competency has been convincingly demonstrated by Marion Sandler, president and co-chief executive officer of Golden West Financial Corporation. In an era when the US savings and loan debacle was gobbling up $400 billion of taxpayers' money, Golden West was a sound and successful thrift organization. Marion, a sharp-minded former Wall Street financial analyst, and her husband, Herbert, purchased sleepy Golden West in 1962 when it had only $34 million in assets. By 1990 its assets were over $20 billion, and analysts were forecasting continued growth.

While other thrifts were hotly pursuing junk bonds, risky condominium loans, questionable commercial real estate, and other hot new lending games, Golden West followed a steady, conservative course. They have strict lending standards and, as a consequence, their record of bad loans is phenomenally low. Among a sea of incompetent savings and loan executives, Marion Sandler and her husband are models of competency.

But there is something else. According to a recent article in the *Wall Street Journal,* they do without corporate jets and corporate dining rooms and even corporate receptionists: Visitors to the company's 17-story headquarters are instructed by a placard to announce their own arrival on an old black telephone.

Marion says she does allow herself the extravagance of a chauffeur: It is her husband who handles that extra chore for free.[3] The Sandlers's modest life-style permeates the entire organization. No executives fly first class, including the Sandlers; and they are expected to stay in mid-priced hotels and rent economy cars. Marion Sandler has demonstrated convincingly that it is possible to be highly competent in the financial world while living a modest life-style.

LEARNING TO USE "JUST ENOUGH"

As we apply a theology of enough to the ministry of competency, we should use only enough of our material gifts to do our work in a very competent manner. Let's be specific.

The Way We Dress

It would be nice to say that how we dress does not affect the competency of our work. But to some extent it does. A bank executive who wears old jeans and tennis shoes to work gives out a message to others that can certainly get in the way of doing his or her job well. Similarly, a social worker who works in poverty areas and who dresses extravagantly erects a barrier with his or her clients that reduces the effectiveness of the services delivered. As CEO of a company that publishes books and magazines on environmental, health, and conservation issues, Bob Rodale's dress fits in with the mission of his firm. Even when he is in a group of other businesspeople who dress more formally, he is readily accepted because he is identified with the mission of his organization. However, if he were a banker or Wall Street financier, his present mode of dress would be unacceptable to his peer group. Like it or not, people who dress "differently" than their colleagues frequently are marginalized in the work group.

However, while a banker or financier may need to wear a well-tailored business suit, must it cost $700 or more? Will a less expensive one not do as well? Of course. Must the lapel width of the jacket be exactly the dimension that the fashion industry has prescribed for a given year? Must the tie width and pattern be what is currently "in"? Many so-called bold and innovative businessmen march mindlessly to the drumbeat of the fashion industry. For a few years the "power tie" was yellow, and all the powerful men wore them. Later the "power tie" was red, and all the powerful followed. Although there are some fanatics in the business world who do expect their employees to dress up to the latest dictates of the fashion industry, they are the exception. Most executives rate performance way above style in evaluating their employees. So why overplay the importance of how we dress? A ministry of life-style will lead us to dress well enough to perform our work competently, but no more.

The Cars We Drive

The same principle applies to the cars we drive. An automobile is simply a means of transportation. Period. It should be reliable, safe, and economical. If you spend a lot of time in one, it should also be comfortable enough to permit you to work effectively. In my judgment many cars in the lower price range of all the big producers meet all these requirements. In over forty years of driving, Judy and I have always purchased Fords, Chevrolets, Plymouths, or Honda Civics. We had two Dodge station wagons and one Pontiac. Because I am tall, our cars had to be roomy enough for me to get behind the wheel. Because Judy does more driving than I do in her volunteer work, we have had two cars for most of our married life. One of our two cars is for use on long trips for vacations or to visit family. That one is the only one to have air-conditioning, stereo radio, and cruise control.

It is possible that some people truly need a fancier car in order to carry out their work competently. A real estate salesperson, who is required to transport clients, may need a more expensive car. But most executives do not transport their clients anywhere. They rent limos or company-provided chauffeured cars for such purposes. What, then, is the purpose of owning a BMW or a Cadillac or a Lincoln Continental or a high-priced sports car other than to flaunt one's position or wealth or status? Are we so insecure that we need expensive cars to convince others of our worth as a human being? Would Jesus drive a BMW?

The Houses We Live In

Our homes are also status symbols for many of us. Yet the basic purpose of a home is to provide shelter. Some people use their homes in the performance of their duties. Because I spent a career in sales, our home was used to entertain customers and, when I was a manager, employees.

We also had four children and a grandmother in our household for about twenty years of married life. Accordingly, we purchased houses that were sufficiently roomy for family and friends, but not ostentatious. We have never had central air-conditioning; in our part of the country a few window air-conditioners in key bedrooms take care of most of the unbearable heat we get a few days each summer.

When I was transferred to Bethlehem, Pennsylvania, to be manager of sales, Judy and I were expected to purchase or build a home in an exclusive residential section where most of our top executives lived. I did not see how the location of our home would affect the competency of my work, so we ignored the suggestions and instead built a home in a less expensive location, strictly dictated by the quality of the school system. For over twenty years it has been a fine place to entertain customers, business associates, family, and friends in a relaxed setting.

Today all our children are grown and gone and my mother is in a nursing home. Judy and I share a five-bedroom house that is much too large for our personal needs. I am retired from Bethlehem Steel and only occasionally need to entertain business associates in our home. We are now in the process of buying a smaller house, simply on the basis that what we now have is more than enough for us, except at Christmas and special occasions. For twenty years our home has been the place where our entire family of children and grandchildren gather at least once a year. It is the place where sixteen of us spend about a week under one roof at Christmastime, renewing and strengthening family ties. Moreover, because we built the house for entertaining, we use it frequently to entertain staff or volunteers of community organizations in which Judy serves as a volunteer. The house has become a current and lively issue in our present ministry of life-style. On the one hand, it seems inappropriate for the two of us to be continuing to live in so large a house. On the other hand, it has become a place of gathering for family and friends in a way that a smaller house could not fulfill. How do we balance both concerns?

The clothes we wear, the cars we drive, the homes we live in all make statements about our values. When we accept the notion that these things are the means by which we demonstrate our status in life, and our success in society, we are captives of the world. We are owned by the world, we are of the world. The Bible gives us no hints whatsoever that Jesus needed more than enough of clothes, transportation, or housing to carry out his ministry. In fact, he prayed that we, his followers, would be safe from the captivation of this world's treasures. No, we are called to a theology of enough, in which we live on the low side of whatever range of materialism that is needed to carry out our other ministries effectively.

Let's be very clear: I am *not* implying that material goods are evil and that devout Christians should renounce all "worldly possessions." That is asceticism, and such a philosophy tends to separate faith and daily life. The theology of enough promotes simplicity, not asceticism.

Richard Foster, in *Celebration of Discipline*, makes this distinction: "Simplicity is the only thing that can sufficiently reorient our lives so that possessions can be genuinely enjoyed without destroying us. Without simplicity we will either capitulate to the 'mammon' spirit of this present age, or we will fall into an un-Christian legalistic asceticism. Both are spiritually lethal."[4]

Spirituality clearly enters into our personal decisions about our material possessions. How we deal with them is one more way in which we make a Monday connection.

Corporate Status Symbols

Some status symbols in life come not as the result of our own conscious decisions, but from people who have decided status for us. The places in which we work, the pay we receive, the benefits we are awarded, and the respect we are given are frequently ego-building measures to let everyone know how worthy we are. But do these symbols really help us to do our work better?

Let's start with offices. It is utterly unconscionable the ways in which the offices of major law firms and financial organizations are decorated. Expensive paneling, tailored cabinet work, lush carpeting, rare antique furniture, fresh flowers, top-of-the-line desks and chairs, built-in bars, private toilets equipped with showers, and exquisite artwork. And all for what? To improve the performance of the workers? Not at all. Simply to impress the world, and those who work in the offices, with how important and successful they are.

That image may help to bring in some new and wealthy clients. But are all clients so naive as to believe that the opulence of an office is the measure of the effectiveness of an organization? It certainly has not been true with many of the big Wall Street and savings and loan companies. The money spent on the design and decoration of offices could be used toward corporate gifts in the community or, in the case of law firms, to allow more pro bono legal representation for poor people.

But what can we do when such lavishness is thrust upon us and everyone else seems to enjoy it? Perhaps we can say no to it all, or at least raise some questions. Each time I received a promotion at Bethlehem Steel and was moved to a new office, the people from office design came around and offered suggestions as to how my new office should be redone. The first time it happened, I was flattered and turned the assignment over to the experts completely. Several months later, as I looked around my office with new carpeting, new paint, new draperies, all new furniture, and new plants, I asked myself, "What have we done here?" The office certainly was different, and to some extent it expressed the difference between the previous occupant and myself. But what had really been accomplished? The people in office design were able to justify their jobs, the vendors of carpeting and furniture got nice orders, and the painters were kept busy. But did I perform any better because of the change? I could not see how.

From that time on I dug in my heels with the office design people whenever they wanted to give me a new office. I think they thought I was a slob. Perhaps that is true, but I didn't see the point of spending money on a perfectly fine office just because a new person occupied it. The real shoot-out came when I became manager of sales. My predecessor had been in his newly decorated office for only about six months because his department had been assigned to a new location in the building. For sentimental reasons he asked if he could buy his desk from the company; they agreed. So I inherited a lovely, recently decorated office with only a desk missing.

Around came the office design people, fully prepared to do the whole office over again. "No," I said, "all I need is a new desk." "But you've got to establish your own personality here," they argued. "Here's how we will do that," I replied. "We'll get me a new desk and move the furniture around." They were slightly aghast, but I insisted and that is just what we did. Got a new desk, rearranged the furniture, and presto! a new office was born.

Just as we are called to be good stewards of our own resources, we are also called to exert good stewardship of the resources of the institution in which we work or serve. I believe that a ministry of values requires one to challenge the status symbols that are conferred upon us. I am convinced that most of us can do so without lessening our competency. And, by doing so, we are making a statement of values. We are connecting the words of the Bible, which we hear on Sunday, with the real-life experiences of Monday.

Our Pay

We also need to consider the matter of pay. Top managers in American corporations are strikingly overpaid compared with their counterparts in Europe and the Orient. Sir Peter Walters, who is credited with turning British Petroleum from a stodgy state-owned company into a highly successful private producer, earned $582,000 in 1987. His American counterpart, Lawrence Rawl, CEO of Exxon, earned $5.5 million in that same year. Lee Iacocca, an American hero for his remarkable turnaround at Chrysler, averaged $16 million in compensation in the years 1985 to 1987. His counterpart in Europe, Jacques Calvert, president of Peugeot, also steered his automaking company from the verge of bankruptcy to robust profits. But Calvert, who works in a small office and locks his phone to prevent unauthorized calls, earned about $250,000 in 1987, which is less than 2 percent of Iacocca's compensation.[5]

Victor Dial, an American who heads sales for Peugeot, explains the difference, "In Europe the greed factor is lower than in the US."[6] He cites Loik Le Floch-Prigent as a prime example. Le Floch-Prigent, who led France's state-owned chemical giant, Rhone-Poulenc, to a spectacular recovery, lives in a Spartan apartment complex in a working class neighborhood on the outskirts of Paris and drives a little Renault 5 to work. His average earnings have been about $150,000. It's not that Europeans can live more cheaply than Americans, or that their tax rates are lower. To the contrary, the cost of living is higher than in the United States and personal tax rates are far higher than here.

The same comparisons prevail when we look at the compensation of Japanese and Korean executives. In Japan there is a rule of thumb that the top executive earns no more than ten times the entry level pay. In America, the ratio is over one hundred times the entry level pay. The argument that American management is worth their pay, based on performance, quickly washes away when one compares the success of Japanese and European companies in the global market. The Japanese have displaced the Americans as the largest banking firms in the world. But John Reed, CEO of Citicorp, American's largest bank, earned $972,000 the year his firm *lost* $1.1 billion, while in that same year Kenichi Kamiya, president of Mitsui Bank, earned $280,000 while his company turned in profits of $336 million![7]

THE DEMONIC POWER OF MONEY

How demonic the power of money and status can be was demonstrated in a survey of affluent Americans conducted by Ernst and Young and Yankelovich, Clancy Shulman in 1989. The average household income for those surveyed was $194,000 and their net assets were $775,000. Although this level of the American population represents only 2 percent of the nation, they control nearly one-third of discretionary income. Incredible as it may seem, 40 percent of the group do not feel financially secure, and 20 percent don't even feel they are financially well off. In terms of priorities in life, the majority place personal success and money above family.[8] These people are owned by the world, and money is their god.

Despite the claim, performance is not the real reason for higher salaries in the United States. Perhaps it is greed. At the least it is a catering to the need for status to prove worth. And therein lies the real problem: worth.

In an ideal world people would be compensated based on their worth to society.[9] We are not in an ideal world. Is Lee Iacocca's $16 million a year in compensation worth the equivalent of one thousand teachers or nurses? How does one equate the millions per year made by pop music artists with the pitifully low salaries of social workers? It is futile to try to make sense out of the way the world compensates people financially. All we say is that, based on worth to society, people are not compensated fairly. The problem is, however, that those who are highly paid are all too ready to believe in their own worth. And that's where they become "of the world." Do we make money or does money make us?

WEALTH AND THE KINGDOM OF GOD

One of the most troubling discourses of Jesus for those who are wealthy occurs when Jesus is approached by a wealthy young man who asks what good thing he must do to get eternal life. Jesus reminds him of the commandments. "All these I have kept," the young man said. "What do I still lack?" To this Jesus answered, "If you want to be perfect, go, sell your possessions and give to the poor, and you will have treasure in heaven. Then come, follow me." The young man went away sadly. Turning to his disciples, Jesus said, "I tell you the truth, it is hard for a rich man to enter the kingdom of heaven" (Matthew 19:16–24 NIV).

Why is it hard for a rich person to enter heaven? Simply because the lure of money is so strong that it is difficult to keep from making it one's god. Some wealthy people, of course, have not become hooked on their wealth, and use it in absolute service to others. But for those multitudes of wealthy whose security is in their money, the way to heaven is blocked by their faith in a false god. Jesus emphasizes this point by adding, "Again I tell you, it is easier for a camel to go through the eye of a needle than for a rich man to enter the kingdom of God." Some Bible scholars have tried to soften these words by offering other interpretations of the original words "camel" and "needle," but most scholars insist that we have the right meaning of Jesus' words before us. Jesus meant to say that God's kingdom is not based on wealth; therefore wealth alone is an impossible qualification for entry into God's kingdom.

In this world wealth does open up doors. Wealth gets us into exclusive neighborhoods, restricted clubs, the finest hotels and restaurants, the best universities, and the most desirable seats in theaters and sporting arenas. Wealth does that, and wealthy people quickly become accustomed to getting where they want to go by means of their wealth. To which Jesus says, it is impossible to use wealth as the means to enter the kingdom of God.

Jesus' disciples were astonished at these words and asked, "Who then can be saved?" Jesus' reply was that it is impossible for any human to save himself or herself, "but with God all things are possible" (Matthew 19:25–26 NIV). It is God alone, with infinite mercy, who saves. No one can prove to God his or her worthiness to be saved.

How does all this relate to the issue of high levels of compensation in some sectors of American society? It is possible for us to eschew wealth by refusing to accept high compensation for our work. I once considered refusing a pay raise as a means of making a statement of values. In the end I didn't do it—partly out of a lack of courage, and partly out of a realization that it would make absolutely no difference in the way my large corporation viewed compensation. Yet there are those saints who forego opportunities for wealth in order to serve humankind: doctors who work in poverty areas, lawyers who represent the poor, clergy who serve small congregations, teachers who seek out the poorest school districts in which to work. These people make impressive statements about the values of their lives. But what about those of us who, for whatever reason, find ourselves in the institutions of society where the compensation system is totally market driven? What about those who have inherited wealth? What about those entrepreneurs who find themselves enormously successful in their business ventures? For these wealthy the task of resisting the demonic power of money becomes crucial. It is here that Christians must make certain that they are "in the world, but not of the world."

Christians, no matter what their circumstances, must use the money they have and not be used by it. As we have seen, giving money away is the most obvious means of using it. One statistic from the last chapter emphasizes the demonic way in which the wealthy can be used by their money: Independent Sector reports that their 1987 study of giving in America revealed that "households that gave 2 percent or more of their income to charity had a lower average household income than households that gave less than 2 percent of their income."[10] Would it be wrong to conclude that the more money we have, the more difficult it is to be released from its grip on our lives?

STATUS

Another way we can carry out a ministry of values where we work is by rejecting the status that is implicit in the hierarchical organizations of American society. If the executive vice president is entitled to be addressed as "Mr." or "Ms.," then so, too, should the shipping clerk and the data processor. Respect should be given to all, without regard to their position in the organizational chart.

The Japanese have taught American business leaders a lesson in this regard. Treating all people with respect and erasing as many lines of distinction as possible between employees pays off in productivity. In most Japanese companies the managers eat in the same lunch rooms as the workers. At Bethlehem Steel we used to have four levels of eating facilities for employees: officers, senior managers, middle managers, and "ordinary" people. Until hard times hit the steel industry, the first three groups had table service, while the "ordinary" people had to line up for cafeteria-style eating.

When I became manager of sales, I was assigned a new parking stall in the company garage. I had been on the second level of the garage, with other assistant managers. Now, I was told, I would be moved down to the first level, where all the other managers had their cars parked. My refusal caused a bit of consternation, which ultimately ended up in the personnel department. I argued that I thought such status symbols were unnecessary and, in some cases, counterproductive. For that I was labeled a "prima donna." But from then on, when people asked me about why I still parked with lesser-level employees, I frankly told them that I thought our company's addiction to status symbols was foolish. It didn't change the system, but it did cause people to think!

PROCLAIMING OUR SOCIAL VALUES

Our ministry of values also compels us to be up front in sharing the social values we respect and in challenging those which we feel are destructive. As Christians we affirm life. This means that we must be supportive of efforts to give all our citizens an equal opportunity to develop their God-given talents to their fullest extent. Those who, by virtue of their race, sex, color of skin, or physical disability, do not have an equal chance to succeed must be helped to develop to their greatest potential.

Why? Because any reading of the Bible will reveal God's passionate concern for those who are at a disadvantage. "Defend the cause of the weak and fatherless," says the Psalmist. "Maintain the rights of the poor and oppressed. Rescue the weak and needy; deliver them from the hand of the wicked" (Psalm 83:3–4 NIV). Psalm 72 speaks of the responsibility of the king to bring justice:

> He will defend the afflicted among the people and save the children of the needy; he will crush the oppressor. . . . He will deliver the needy who cry out, the afflicted who have no one to help. He will take pity on the weak and the needy and save the needy from death. He will rescue them from oppression and violence, for precious is their blood in his sight. (Psalm 72:4, 12–14 NIV)

When we hear comments that blacks or Hispanics or women don't deserve special opportunities to advance in life, we need to speak out. The plain fact is that our society is still racist and sexist, which has to be an affront to God, the creator. We may not have all the answers as to how problems of discrimination can be eliminated, but that does not disqualify us from continuing to say that discrimination is wrong.

Similarly, we must be forthright on issues of the environment. "The earth is the Lord's, and everything in it, the world, and all who live in it" (Psalm 24:1 NIV). We cannot continue to deplete the resources of this planet, to foul its air and pollute its waters. We know what the effects of environmental irresponsibility will mean to future generations. We also have most of the technical ability to reverse this deterioration of the environment. The ministry of values compels us to live simply and to raise our voices in concern over what is happening to the earth.

THE NATION'S CHILDREN

A critical issue on which Christians must seriously express their values has to do with what is happening to our children. Whereas poverty once was a serious concern for the elderly, it has become an increasingly critical factor for the nation's children. To put it bluntly, the old are getting richer at the expense of the young. Older folks can vote; children cannot. And this is making a difference in the distribution of our nation's resources.

Consider these facts: In 1959, 22.4 percent of all Americans had incomes below the federally defined poverty level. However, 35 percent of those over sixty-five were in poverty, as were 26.9 percent of all children under eighteen. By 1987 the situation had dramatically reversed for the elderly. While the national poverty rate was 13.5 percent, the elderly's rate was only 12.2 percent. The rate for children under eighteen, however, stood at 20 percent. These comparisons are based only on cash incomes. When we add non cash supplements such as Medicare, food stamps, and housing subsidies, the number of elderly poor falls to about 5 percent. "Poverty among the elderly, as measured by the poverty index and adjusted for non-money income has virtually disappeared," says James Schultz, professor of economics at Brandeis University.[11]

Income is not the only way in which the elderly have improved their lot in life. They have enjoyed great financial benefit from the sharp rises in real estate values and other equities that have taken place in the past twenty years. During the 1950s the number of owner-occupied housing almost doubled from 17 million to 33 million.[12] The value of much of that real estate today is so high that younger families can no longer afford to buy homes. In the mid-1950s a thirty-year-old person could carry the payments on a medium-priced house, including taxes and insurance on 14 percent of the person's median gross income. Today it would take 41 percent. Furthermore, as more people move into retirement years, there will be fewer workers to support the Social Security system— which means younger people will have to pay higher taxes to keep the system sound. Both Social Security and Medicare have helped the elderly to keep their wealth intact by easing the drain on their assets.

Social Security was originally designed to be a type of safety net for the elderly. Today many elderly really do not need that safety net, but Social Security has become an entitlement, meaning everyone can have it. To a degree, these entitlements are taking money from struggling young families and giving it to the comfortable old. "The United States has become the first society in history in which the poorest group in the population are the children, not the aged," observes Senator Moynihan of New York. "A person six years or younger has seven times a greater likelihood of being poor than a person sixty-five or older."[13]

How can this be happening? It's simple. The elderly are a politically astute group. They can vote. The young cannot. The elderly have a powerful, well-financed lobby in the form of the American Association of Retired Persons. The young do not. So when Ronald Reagan or George Bush or any other president tries to cut back on spending, where does the axe fall? Not upon those who can exert strong political pressure. It's the kids who get the axe.

It has been said that the quality of a nation can be measured by the way it cares for its elderly and its children. Should we be pleased that our elderly are now fairly well cared for—at the expense of our children?

If we put aside for the moment the injustice of what is happening and look strictly at the self-interest of our nation, what we are doing is suicidal. Our children are the physical capital of the country. They are our future. Yet infant mortality, children without health insurance, homelessness, teenage pregnancy, chemical abuse, and illiteracy are all on the rise. "Today's poor children will become the defective raw materials for the economic base of the next century," says Representative George Miller of the House Select Committee on Children, Youth and Families.[14] Our nation will pay heavily for what we are doing today. We are mortgaging our future.

Apart from the national self-interest, there is a moral issue. We are not saving "the children of the needy," as the Psalmist reminds us (Psalm 72:4 NIV). What is going on in our country today is an ugly evil in the sight of God.

It is time that Christians assert their values by speaking out on this injustice. More likely than not, we will be speaking to ourselves. I am approaching sixty-five years of age, so I think I know where the elderly are coming from. We are children of the Great Depression. We know what it is like to be in want. We have enough mistrust of the system to fear that another depression may occur within our lifetime. We are also the products of an ethic that says we should not be dependent on others. We are to provide for ourselves. We do not want to be dependent upon our own children in our old age if we can possibly avoid it.

On top of all this, we see that people are living longer, well beyond the years of gainful employment. So we wonder how much we must put aside in order to make sure that we do not outlive our assets. We, too, have been hooked by the god of personal security. We worry. We are afraid of the future. Yet Jesus says,

> "Therefore, I tell you, do not worry about your life, what you will eat or drink; or about your body, what you will wear. . . . And why do you worry about clothes? See how the lilies of the field grow. They do not labor or spin. Yet I tell you that not even Solomon in all his splendor was dressed like one of these. If that is how God clothes the grass of the field, which is here today and tomorrow is thrown into the fire, will he not much more clothe you, O you of little faith? So do not worry, saying, 'What shall we eat?' or 'What shall we drink?' or 'What shall we wear?' For the pagans run after all these things and your heavenly Father knows that you need them. But seek first his kingdom and his righteousness, and all these things will be given to you as well. Therefore do not worry about tomorrow, for tomorrow will worry about itself. Each day has enough trouble of its own." (Matthew 6:25, 28–34 NIV)

Christians have the opportunity to make a powerful demonstration of their faith in those words. We must break away from a culture that is hung up on security. Our nation has become obsessed with an expectation that life should be totally safe and perfect. If only we eat the right foods, we will never get cancer or heart disease. Every baby born should be perfect and if it is not, we sue the obstetrician. If we are injured in a fall, we sue the owner of the property. If we build enough bombs, we will never have war. If we accumulate enough assets, we will never need the help of another person. It is unrealistic to expect life to be risk-free. Not only that, but God actually asks us to risk. God asks us to trust that we will be provided for. Otherwise, our security itself becomes our god. We worship security.

How might all this play out in our ministry of values? First, we need to let go of our obsession for security by generously giving to others. God does not expect us to be irresponsible in providing for ourselves, but since we will never know for certain how much money is needed for a secure future, we should take greater risks against that future in order to give to those who are in need now.

Fund-raising organizations are coming up with creative ways in which people can commit to planned giving through their wills, deferred gift annuities, unitrusts, insurance policies, and other means without totally surrendering all their assets prior to death.

We can demonstrate our ministry of values by trying to change the system. In 1988 Congress ran into a buzz saw when it tried to fund a catastrophic health plan for the elderly through a progressive tax on those in the Medicare system, with the wealthiest of the elderly paying the highest surtax. The wrath of the wealthy elderly burst forth in incredible fury and in a few months' time Congress backed off the plan.

I think that the approach of Congress was right, even though it would hurt me in retirement years. Why shouldn't those who have enough income to support the funding of the program help pay for those who do not? Why should this be passed on to our children? I made my feelings known to a group of former Bethlehem Steel associates who are now retired, and they thought I was insane. They wanted it to come out of Social Security revenues, which our children are paying. I find it strange indeed that the retirees who fought the hardest against the funding plan are the ones who still maintain memberships in private golf clubs and still drive big cars. Something's got to change!

We need to support our children by pressing for programs that assure all of them of good nutrition, shelter, clothing, education, and a nurturing family environment in which they can develop into wholesome, healthy human beings. There is no indication that this can be accomplished through charitable giving and volunteerism alone. The role of government is to do what is needed if it can be done in no other way by no other means. Regardless of our political philosophy, we must press for government to get our children out of poverty and sickness and despair and turn around what has been happening to them in the past ten years.

THE ROLE OF CHURCHES

What can be the role of churches in helping Christians to "live on the low side"? First, we must expand the meaning of stewardship. Stewardship is not confined to the narrow understanding of how much money and time we give to the church. Stewardship has to deal with how we use *all* our money and *all* our time. The church needs to work hard at teaching this.

Second, with respect to values as expressed through public policy, the churches should not rely solely upon the pronouncements of bishops or the resolutions of denominational assemblies. Through educational programs in the congregations, through adult forums on public policy issues, and through encouraging laypeople to become active in the political process, members of congregations can carry out their ministries in society. The chambers of commerce have offered courses in effective politics to help their members bring about change in the public arena. Shouldn't churches do the same?

The ministry of values calls us to be giving people. It also calls us to take the words of God, as revealed in the Old Testament and through the teachings of Jesus, and make them real in our everyday lives. That's our Monday connection. We do this through our style of living, our rejection of the status symbols the world dangles in front of us, our affirmation of life through our care for how people are treated and how our earth is conserved, and our willingness to risk some of our future on behalf of those who are in need now. Christians are liberated people. Our worth has been established at our baptism, and our eternal future is secure. We can witness to those convictions through our ministry of values.

VII

MAKING THE
CONNECTION

CHAPTER 12

Roles and Responsibilities

"Why should rank and file Christians, in the last years of the twentieth century, beg a theologian or a bishop to furnish them with their Christian responsibility? God encounters each person individually to seek personal response. Our world is a gift and a task from God. The initiative is ours." So says Ed Marciniak, one of the Roman Catholic leaders at the National Center for the Laity.[1]

"The Laity must be agents of their own formation." So said the World Council of Churches in 1974.[2]

In its earliest years the Christian church was entirely a lay movement. The followers of Jesus were clearly not the church professionals of their time. They were very ordinary people. The spread of Christianity in those first three crucial centuries was due entirely to the initiatives taken by laypeople, both men and women. The history of the Christian church is studded with examples of how lay-initiated movements provided new and exciting growth for the church universal.

The monastic movement, which had its beginnings in the fourth century, was initially a lay movement and was not integrated into the hierarchal structure of the church for several centuries. To this day the Franciscan order is lay.

When the names of Luther and Calvin come to mind as one speaks of the Reformation, we need to remind ourselves that only one of them, Luther, was of the clergy. Moreover, the Reformation would never have succeeded had it not been for the initiatives of many laypeople in France, Germany, Holland, Switzerland, and England who published religious books on the theological issues of the Reformation.

Hendrik Kraemer points out that the struggle between the "free churches" in the Anglo-Saxon countries, which were largely under lay leadership, and the "established" church of the country, greatly influenced the democratic principles of Western civilization. He writes, "Modern democracy owes, as to its origins, as much to these Bible-centered developments in the Christian Church as to the totally different assault of the Enlightenment."[3]

The Quaker movement began as a lay initiative and remains so today, although it has structures similar to the clergy-led denominations.

Much missionary work in the New World was the result of lay initiatives. Nikolaus von Zinzendorf, a layman, brought the Moravians to America.

Ever-expanding lay initiatives in the nineteenth century resulted in the formation of the YMCA, the YWCA, and the World Student Christian Federation. Many organizations and movements in the country today, devoted to the needs of society, have been started by laypeople. The impetus behind many of these organizations was the realization that a need existed in society to which the church organizations were not responding.

As we reflect on the many lay-initiated movements within the history of the Christian church, it is important to note that they arose in order to fulfill the mission of the church, not to thwart it. Hendrik Kraemer points out, "It cannot be too strongly stressed that these great expressions of Christian lay-vision and sense of responsibility have performed *vicariously* a task which, in principle, lies within the calling of the Church, but for which the Church as a whole was too clumsy, too defensive and empty of real vision."[4]

We can give thanks for those many laypeople throughout the ages who, seeing that the institution church was failing to carry out its mission, took their own initiative to be the agents of God in meeting the needs of the time. Their stories bear out the truth that God's work in the world is not solely dependent on religious institutions. God acts through the church universal, particularly when the religious institutions of the times become ossified. The issue we need to raise in these times is: Are our religious institutions capable of helping their members make the Monday connection, or must it be purely a lay initiative?

The principle that all baptized Christians have been called into ministry in their daily lives is universally accepted among all American denominations. While there may be all kinds of theological differences which keep the denominations apart, the principle of the universal priesthood is not one of them.

In preparation for writing this book, I secured copies of the official documents or mission statements of the major American denominations to determine what they had to say about the ministry of laypeople in and to the world. Without exception, the rhetoric was there. In some cases it was bold rhetoric. But when I checked with members of those denominations, I found that—without exception—the reality was otherwise.

The experience of the Roman Catholic church serves as a good illustration. It begins with Vatican II.

In 1963 the Second Vatican Council delivered to the church and to the world a document that gave great promise for the role of the laity. In what many regard as the most imposing achievement of the Council, *The Dogmatic Constitution on the Church*, discussion of the people of God preceded discussion of the hierarchal structure of the church.[5] This reversal of the usual order of church documents was in itself a sharp departure from the past. But what was said about the laity was even more unusual.

Chapter IV of *The Dogmatic Constitution on the Church* is entitled, "The Laity." Laity is defined as all the faithful baptized, "except those in holy orders and those in a religious state sanctioned by the church."[6] The document, in part, says this about the laity:

> But the laity, by their very vocation, seek the kingdom of God by engaging in temporal affairs and by ordering them according to the plan of God. They live in the world, that is, in each and in all of the secular professions and occupations. They live in the ordinary circumstances of family and social life, from which the very web of their existence is woven.
>
> They are called there by God so that by exercising their proper function and being led by the spirit of the gospel they can work for the sanctification of the world from within, in the manner of leaven. In this way they can make Christ known to

others, especially by the testimony of a life resplendent in
faith, hope, and charity. The layman is closely involved in tem-
poral affairs of every sort. It is, therefore, his special task to
illumine and organize these affairs in such a way that they may
always start out, develop, and persist according to Christ's
mind, to the praise of the Creator and the Redeemer.[7]

A significant part of the material that follows deals with the role
of the laity in the affairs of the church. This section, in itself, was
seen as revolutionary. But then the Council turns to the role of the
laity in the world.

Therefore, by their competence in secular fields and by their
personal activity, elevated from within by the grace of Christ,
let them labor vigorously so that by human labor, technical
skill, and civic culture created goods may be perfected for the
benefit of every last man, according to the design of the Creator and the light of His Word. Let them work to see that created goods are more fittingly distributed among men, and that
such goods in their own way lead to general progress in human and Christian liberty. . . .

Moreover, let the laity also by their combined efforts remedy
any institutions and conditions of the world which are custom-
arily an inducement to sin, so that all such things may be con-
formed to the norms of justice and may favor the practice of
virtue rather than hinder it. By so doing, laymen will imbue
culture and human activity with moral values. They will better
prepare the field of the world for the seed of the Word of
God. . . .

For even in secular affairs there is no human activity which can
be withdrawn from God's dominion.[8]

Faithful Roman Catholic laity throughout the world, and particularly in the United States, were electrified by this strong affirmation of what they themselves had concluded: They have a special
Christian ministry in and to the world. (Please note that the Monday ministries of competency, presence, ethics, change, and life-
style are all referred to in this text.)

How would the rhetoric of Vatican II be converted into reality?
American laity waited. And waited.

Changes did occur. In the parishes, laypeople—mostly men—
began to assume greater roles within the worship services and in

the governance of parish matters. But, as for the ministry of the laity in and to the world, there was silence.

Finally, in December 1977, a group of American Catholic laity and clergy met in Chicago to share their frustration over the failure of the Vatican II documents to be fully implemented. They shared a particular concern that greater lay involvement in parish activities was, by inference, depreciating lay ministries in the world.

From this meeting came a document signed by forty-seven conference participants. Now known as *A Chicago Declaration of Christian Concern*, this document called the church and all faithful members to make real the challenging rhetoric of Vatican II. The declaration gives high praise to the forceful teaching of Vatican II on the ministry of the laity, but bitterly claims "in recent years it seems to have all but vanished from the consciousness and agendas of many sectors within the church."[9]

In particular, the declaration notes,

> It is our experience that a wholesome and significant movement within the Church—the involvement of lay people in many Church ministries—has led to a devaluation of the unique ministry of lay men and women. The tendency has been to see lay ministry as involvement in some church related activity, e.g., religious education, pastoral care for the sick and elderly, or readers in church on Sunday. Thus lay ministry is seen as the laity's participation in work traditionally assigned to priests or sisters.

> We recognize the new opportunities opened up to the laity to become deacons, but believe that in the long run such programs will be a disaster if they create the impression that only in such fashion do the laity mainly participate in the mission of the Church.[10]

The closing paragraph of the declaration brings the concerns of the writers into sharp focus:

> In the last analysis, the Church speaks to and acts upon the world through her laity. Without a dynamic laity conscious of its personal ministry to the world, the Church, in effect, does not speak or act. No amount of social action by priests and religious can ever be an adequate substitute for enhancing lay responsibility. The absence of lay initiative can only take us down the road to clericalism. We are deeply concerned that

so little energy is devoted to encouraging and arousing lay
responsibility for the world. The Church must constantly be
reformed, but we fear that the almost obsessive preoccupation
with the Church's structures and processes has diverted attention from the essential question: reform for what purpose? It
would be one of the great ironies of history if the era of Vatican II which opened the windows of the Church to the world
were to close with a Church turned in upon herself.[11]

The Chicago Declaration received such an avalanche of positive
response from Catholics throughout the country that the National
Center for the Laity was formed to keep alive the discussion of the
church/world issue. The National Center for the Laity has no official
standing within the Catholic church. It receives no institutional
church funding. Apart from its board of directors, composed of
both laity and clergy, the National Center has no chapters, no formal membership and no required dues. It has never had a paid
staff. Its bimonthly newsletter, *Initiatives*, its national conferences,
its books and publications are all the result of volunteer time and
contributions.[12] Its pamphlets on the spirituality of work within
various occupations are exceptionally fine pieces of work.

Through the National Center for the Laity, Roman Catholics
from various parts of the country have been able to network with
each other. Through a series of national consultations, they continue their efforts to steer the massive hierarchy of their church in
the directions so clearly articulated by Vatican II.

However, when a typical Roman Catholic layperson is asked
about what the significance of Vatican II has been for the laity, the
answer invariably will be that laity are more involved in the worship
and organizational matters of the local parish. They are generally
unaware of Vatican II's strong call for the ministry of the laity in and
to the world.

Unfortunately, that is typical of what has come out of the pronouncements of the other major denominations in America. I have
yet to run into one Episcopal layperson who is aware that a recently
revised Canon III.1 reads, "Of the Ministry of all baptized members: Each diocese shall make provisions for the development and
affirmation of the ministry of all baptized persons in the church and
in the world."[13]

In June 1987 the American Baptist churches, at their biennial meeting in Pittsburgh, adopted a wonderful statement of concern, entitled, "The Ministry of the Whole People of God; Living Our Faith Where We Are."[14] It is a remarkable document, rich with excellent "opportunities" to affirm and equip lay members for ministry in daily life. Unfortunately, I have yet to meet one American Baptist layperson who has ever seen this document, much less studied it.

The same problem exists with respect to the *Book of Discipline* of the United Methodist church; the "Pronouncement on Empowering the Laity for Ministry" of the United Church of Christ; the Southern Baptist's foundational document, "The Ministry of the Laity"; and the "Declaration of Ministry" adopted by the former Lutheran Church in America.[15] Each of them had fine rhetoric about ministry in daily life, but it is difficult to find laypeople who have heard of the pronouncements, much less experienced the implementation of them within their congregations.

At their best, these documents on the role of the laity have brought laypeople into greater participation in the worship and organizational activities of their churches. We end up training laypeople to do what pastors do: participate in worship, teach, administer congregational affairs, visit the sick, bring in new members, and raise more money. All these activities are necessary, and it is good more laypeople are doing them; but, as the Roman Catholic laity have pointed out, if this is all that is meant by the ministry of the laity, we have turned the church in upon itself.

The principle of the universal priesthood has the potential for being a church-transforming power. Yet, as Hendrik Kraemer points out, "To the present day it rather fulfills the role of a flag than of an energizing, vital principle."[16] Reviewing the history of Christianity from the time of Constantine to today, Kraemer concludes, "For the greater part of its history, the church has provided little place in its thinking for expressing the meaning of the laity in the divine economy of salvation in the world and in the economy of the church."[17]

History has shown that, if left to the church professionals alone, there will never be much of a ministry in daily life for most of the Christians in America. Putting aside a small minority of ordained ministers who are threatened by the principle of a universal priesthood, most church professionals support a ministry of the laity in principle but do not know *how* to equip people for ministry in daily life. The reason is perfectly understandable.

For the ordained ministers and many of the lay professionals, the church institution has been the center of their universe. They have been raised in the church, attended church-related colleges, graduated from seminaries of their church, received calls to congregations of the church, and perhaps advanced into positions within the bureaucratic structures of their denominations. They know what ministry *in* the church looks like. Accordingly, they have an idea of how the laity can do ministry in the church. Since they are largely unfamiliar with the institutions of business, law, medicine, research science, government, the media, and the scores of others that comprise our complex society, it is only natural that they do not tend to think of ministry in and to nonchurch institutions. Bishops and other church leaders commend those clergy who have active lay involvement in their congregations. No such commendations come as the result of equipping laity for ministry in the world.

If congregations are to affirm, equip, and support laypeople for ministry in and to the world, both the clergy and the lay members must have a partnership in making that happen.

Together we need to work on our language. We unnecessarily use the terms clergy and laity in ways that imply there are two types of Christians in this world. Since the church has a mission to which all its members are called, should we not refer to "the people of God" or a similar inclusive phrase? Similarly, the term "ministry in daily life" includes all the members, not just one group. Because of its past usage, we should discontinue the term "lay ministry" completely. For too many years it has been used to describe the activities of laypeople exclusively in the life and worship of a congregation. If it is necessary to identify a type of ministry that is generally not available to clergy, then "ministry of the laity" is perhaps the best term.

The Statement of Concern adopted by the American Baptist Churches at their 1987 biennial meeting recommended that the words "call" and "vocation" apply to all believers.[18] This is very important, as I discovered in doing the research for my book *In Search of Faithfulness*.[19] It was quite apparent that those laypeople who felt "called" to their present jobs had a clear understanding of their ministry and their identity.

The term "church vocations" is, therefore, unhelpful. All Christians have a vocation, a calling, to ministry in daily life. We respond to that calling through various roles—as worker, parent, spouse, citizen, friend, and so on. If we mean to say that a person is fulfilling his or her vocation by working in the church institution, let's talk about "church occupations."

Let's stop using the term "dedicated layperson" when referring to one who is very active in church work alone. A dedicated layperson is one who carries out ministry in all aspects of life. When a congregation is without a pastor, we frequently refer to it as a "vacant congregation"—as if the nonordained don't exist!

The intent of watching our language is not to become anticlerical or to diminish the importance of ordained ministry. Ministry is not a zero sum game. To lift up the ministry of all the people of God is not to lower the ministry of the clergy. Rather, it is *multiplying* ministry.

ROLES AND RESPONSIBILITIES

If we are to make a successful Monday connection, both laity and clergy must have specific roles and responsibilities. Laypeople must claim their own ministries. While friends may help us to see where our ministries are already at work, each of us must assume responsibility for those ministries. I cannot expect someone else to tell me how and to what extent I am to balance my ministries to my family, my occupation, my community, and my church. I must take that initiative. Clergy can play a very supportive role in our efforts to have Sunday and Monday connect. This does not mean that clergy have more work to do; it simply means that clergy may work differently.

The Christian church has a rhythm of coming together (congregating) on Sunday for worship, study, renewal, and inspiration *so that* the people of God can go out on Monday and be the church in the world. This can happen effectively if laypeople and clergy work together at the affirming, equipping, and supporting of all members for their ministries in daily life.

AFFIRMING

How can Monday ministries be affirmed in the Sunday worship service? Clearly, a sermon that connects the Scripture lessons of the day with real-life situations in the Monday world is an important fundamental.

Reinhold Niebuhr said that every sermon should be preached with the Bible in one hand and the morning newspaper in the other. Clergy who spend time listening to their lay members talk about their weekday experiences will have plenty of sermon illustrations upon which to draw. This is why pastors are encouraged to call on their members at their places of employment. The purpose simply is to learn what people do in the world—not one word about congregational activities, just listening to peoples' stories of what they do and the problems they face. If it is not possible to visit while the person is working, perhaps the pastor can share lunch where the member usually eats. For a pastor to visit a member where he or she works is, in itself, a very affirming action. But it also equips the pastor to preach affirming sermons.

In somewhat the same way that the early church took over pagan holiday practices in celebrating Christmas, we can make the Monday connection by observing worldly holidays within the Sunday worship setting. Labor Day Sunday can focus on ministry in the workplace. People can be asked to dress for the worship service in the same clothes they will wear on Monday. Some churches have asked people to bring symbols of their daily work to place on the altar at the time of the offering. Tools, textbooks, pocket calculators, date books, driver's licenses, tea towels, chalk, pots and pans, lunch pails, and scores of other symbols of occupation can be placed on the altar (to be reclaimed after the service, of course).

The Sunday before election day can stress the ministry we have to community. We can lift up the ministry of parenthood on Mother's Day and Father's Day. We can remember the birthdays of those who have ministered to society through their service to the world: Florence Nightingale, Martin Luther King, Albert Einstein, J. S. Bach, Benjamin Franklin, and others. It is not helpful, however, to have an annual "Layman's Sunday." That is tokenism. Every Sunday is for laypeople. It is the day to prepare for ministry in the world.

"MINISTRY IN . . ."

In the same way that congregations affirm those who carry out their ministries within the church, they can also recognize and affirm ministries in the world. Many congregations officially install their newly elected church council members during a worship service. The same thing holds true for Sunday school teachers and those who go out on every-member visits for fund-raising. These people are usually called up to the altar during a worship service and commissioned by the pastor to carry out their ministries in the congregation. Usually the congregation is asked if they will support these laypeople and pray for their ministries.

Exactly the same approach is taken in our congregation with respect to peoples' ministries in the world. We combine the affirmation service with a series of educational sessions in what we call the "Ministry in . . ." series. Here's how it worked in our most recent series.

Because of the increasing crisis in American education, we decided to call together all the members of our congregation who were in any way related to the field of education. We can easily identify such persons because our congregational directory identifies the names, addresses, and "occupations" of each baptized member. The term occupation refers to what primarily occupies each member's time. Paid jobs are listed, but also the grades that students are in and the volunteer work or activities of those who do not work for pay, such as homemakers and the retired. This way of recording our members is, in itself, another way of affirming peoples' ministries in daily life.

We wrote to about sixty members who were in the field of education—teachers, principals, a school district superintendent, college professors, tutors, school board members, foster parents, day-care workers, and others. We asked them to join in a four-week forum series on the crisis in American education. On four successive Sunday mornings, during the one-hour period for church school, we asked four different panels from the group to discuss issues of concern to those in the field of education. Then, on the fourth Sunday, during the worship service, we recognized the ministries of our people in education.

From the sixty letters that went out, about forty-five responded. In addition, the sessions were open to other members of the congregation. In all, about sixty people attended.

The first session dealt with what we should expect from our education system. We heard from a parent, a student, a college educator, a business employer, and a school district superintendent.

On the second Sunday a panel discussed the education of children with special needs: those who are gifted and those with learning disabilities. Should children with special needs be "mainstreamed" or segregated? The third topic dealt with values: where are children taught values? Is it the basic responsibility of the home, the school, or the church? The public school teachers related with dismay the restrictions that are placed upon them not to teach values in the classroom. On the final Sunday a panel presented ideas of what needed to be done in the years ahead to provide our society with quality education.

Following the final session, those who felt comfortable doing so joined in the processional during our worship service. They sat as a group in the front rows of the church, and were called up to the altar for a service of affirmation. As a part of the commissioning service, the congregation was asked to rise and indicate they would support these, our ministers in the field of education, with our prayers and encouragement. Thus, we "commissioned" members of our congregation to be our ministers in the field of education in our community.

We have done similar series with those in the field of health care, business, law, homemaking, public service, and the media. The objective is to offer every member the opportunity to be affirmed in their ministries in life within the worship service of the congregation.

OTHER WAYS OF AFFIRMING

Congregations can take simple steps to affirm the ministry of all the members. The Sunday bulletin can say that the ministers of the congregation are all the members; the pastors and other staff people are listed below by name. Some congregations have large bulletin boards on which the church secretary tacks daily newspaper clippings that mention the activities of any of the members. The bulletin board usually carries a heading, such as "Our People in Ministry." The congregational newsletter can carry an article by or about the ministry of one of the members. The congregation to which I belong has adopted an organizing principle of "the Holy Spirit empowers us for ministry in daily life." This message appears on all our congregational stationery, envelopes, bulletins, newsletters, and even our coffee mugs. Many congregations have special banners that hang in the worship area, proclaiming ministry in and to the world in various ways.

We have found that prayers written by laypeople have been an important element of the worship service. And, of course, laypeople assist in many parts of the worship service.

EQUIPPING

Equipping deals primarily with the question of "How?" How do I express my faith in the workplace or community? How can I develop better skills for ministry? How can I relate biblical and theological principles to the problems and decisions I face in daily life? How can I discover where my talents for ministry are strongest?

I cannot overemphasize the importance of creating occasions and events where people can discuss the experiences of life within the environment of the Christian community. Auburn Seminary of New York City has designed an excellent course on "Faith in Daily Life." During the course of designing and field testing the program, an outside educator was asked to evaluate the material and process. The evaluation report reads in part:

> One discovery has been that the invitation to laypeople to think about their faith in relationship to their daily lives is a new opportunity. Generally the church has not invited them to reflect in any sustained way the meaning of religious faith for the activities on which they spend most of their time and energy—work, family, and community life. The laypeople . . . have been pleasantly surprised by the approach of this project, especially on its emphasis in hearing from them about their experiences rather than telling them what to think or do. And they find gratifying the opportunity to put two different kinds of meaningful experience together: what happens on Sunday and what happens the rest of the week.[20]

With respect to clergy, the evaluation report says,

> Clergy, we find, are quite open to an approach of this kind, but they have few ideas of their own about how to structure and lead such an opportunity. Their theological education has

not prepared them to help laypeople understand the full ministry of God's people and to support that ministry at the parish
level. Generally, the kind of teaching and educational leadership that is modeled in seminary programs, patterns of Bible
study, for instance, is not effective in educational programs for
lay adults.[21]

SHARING EXPERIENCES

The emerging models for equipping people for ministry in daily
life all point toward the teaching method of gathering people together around a common need or concern about ministry in daily
life, encouraging them to discuss their own experiences relating to
such concerns and then, with the aid of a pastor or one skilled in
theology, jointly working through the appropriate connections between faith and daily life.

The several examples of our "Monday Connection" group cited
earlier in this book is a program that has been working well in our
congregation. The "Ministry in . . ." series is another type of program in which people share experiences. In connection with his visits to the workplace, our pastor received a request from a group of
our members who work for the same company that he have a
monthly Bible study with them at noon in the company cafeteria.
The Bible study is to relate to the experiences of the workplace.

The program designed by Auburn Theological Seminary consists of a weekend retreat, followed by six one-night sessions in
which participants deal with their faith-life connections. It can be
secured for congregational use by contacting the Seminary in New
York. A similar but more extensive program called "Connections"
is available from the Evangelical Lutheran Church in America.[22]

SKILLS DEVELOPMENT

Adult education periods provide excellent opportunities to deal
with the how-to's of ministry in daily life. A number of suggested
courses have already been mentioned in earlier chapters: effective
listening, basic counseling skills, first aid, effective politics, ethical
decision making. The case study on Helen, the supervisor who

witnessed to her employees in the office, points up a need for courses on how to witness to one's faith.

The Montgomery Community Baptist Church of Cincinnati has developed its own School of Lay Ministry, which offers courses on the how-to's of making the Monday connections with Sunday. The Lay School runs alongside more traditional adult education courses. A congregation in Pennsylvania, however, is designing a Center for Faith and Life that will take over the complete post-confirmation education program of the church. The center will have basic, entry-level courses relating to ministry in daily life, and then offer the opportunity for persons to work and study in one of four ministry sectors: occupation, family, community, and church. The plan is to have laypeople design and lead the courses, with pastors providing biblical and theological insights.

Equipping can also come in the form of one-day seminars. A group of congregations in a particular location can sponsor Saturday seminars on faith-life topics for laypeople. For example, a group of congregations in Pennsylvania sponsored a one-day conference at the local college on the topic, "Christians and the Courts." Invitations went out to attorneys and judges in the community to gather to discuss how Christians in the judicial system can carry out their ministries when the whole process is adversarial in nature. A theologian was present to provide insights from his perspective.

Saturday Lenten breakfasts are another opportunity for speakers to present faith-life issues for discussion. Or, as a variation, a downtown Wednesday noon Lenten luncheon series can accomplish the same thing. The opportunities are limitless.

Not enough congregations encourage laypeople to do independent study through book reading. Books were crucial to me when I began to develop my own sense of ministry. Yet, never was a book recommended to me by a parish pastor. Excellent books are available on all aspects of the how-to's of ministry in the world. Some of these are listed in the Bibliography at the end of this book. A number of ecumenical organizations regularly publish periodicals containing excellent faith-life essays for laypeople, as well as announcements of conferences and listings of other lay resources. Among the best are *Laity Exchange, Centering,* and *Lay Communiqué.*[23]

SUPPORT

Throughout this book I have stressed the need for support groups. They can be occupational groups at the place of work; they can be issue-related support groups, such as the one described in Judy's efforts for a new women's prison; thcy can be congregational-based support groups such as our present *koinonia* group; or they can be interest-related support groups such as Parents Without Partners, Alcoholics Anonymous, and the like. While each of these types of groups may have a different focus and agenda, the basic purpose is the same: to provide a place where people can discuss the issues, experiences, and dilemmas of life within the environment of a group of caring friends who share the same commitments to the Christian faith.

Support groups can easily be started by laypeople. There are abundant resources on how to start support groups and nurture their development. Care needs to be taken that they do not become elitist and exclusive in nature, but with good judgment this need not happen.

The congregational functions of affirming, equipping, and supporting people for their ministries in daily life can largely be initiated and carried out by laypeople. The support of the clergy is needed, of course, and their skills are needed for certain types of programs. But a partnership between laypeople and clergy can energize a congregation into a dynamic center for relating Sunday faith to the Monday world.

People who are unfortunate enough to encounter clergy resistance in their congregation can look for an ecumenical groups with which to relate. Several were mentioned in this book. And, as has been true in my own life, self-study can be an avenue to claiming one's ministry. It is often said in the business community "All development is self-development." That advice is also applicable to those of us who hunger for the faith-life connection but receive no encouragement from our congregations. That development depends to a great extent upon our own initiatives.

OUR CALL

We have seen that all American denominations believe in the principle of the universal priesthood of the baptized. They say so in their organizational documents. We have also seen that, at best, most denominations have gone no further in supporting the ministry of the laity than to involve them in church work.

George Gallup tells us that people are less inclined to be members of churches today than they were ten years ago, even though more of them confess a belief in Jesus Christ as the son of God. What people are hungering for, we are told, is the means to relate the experiences of life to their faith. Gallup predicts that if the churches can meet this need, there can be real church growth in the 1990s.[24]

Whether the church institutions of America succeed or fail in meeting this challenge to their very existence, it remains the task of every Christian to respond to God's gracious presence in our own life by being the channels for God to touch the lives of others in the world. For the sake of the world and for the sake of our own spiritual integrity, we need to make the Monday connection.

Notes

Introduction

1. No author, *The Unchurched American—10 Years Later* (Princeton, NJ: Princeton Research Center, 1988), 3.
2. Ari L. Goldman, "Mainline Church Group Is Forced to Retrench," *New York Times*, reprinted in the Allentown, PA *Morning Call* (November 4, 1988): A14.

PART I. THE SUNDAY/MONDAY GAP

Chapter 1. Unconnected

1. No author, *The Unchurched American—10 Years Later* (Princeton, NJ: Princeton Research Center, 1988), 2.
2. Wade Clark Roof and William McKinney, "Denominational America and the New Religion Pluralism," in *Religion in America Today* in *The Annals of the American Academy of Political Science*, edited by Wade Clark Roof (Beverly Hills: Sage Publications, 1985), 29.
3. Robert Wagman, "Ethics: Its Decline and Fall During the Reagan Presidency," the Allentown, PA *Morning Call* (September 4, 1988): A10.
4. Wade Clark Roof and William McKinney, *American Mainline Religion: Its Changing Shape and Future* (New Brunswick, NJ: Rutgers University Press, 1987), 154.
5. Elton Trueblood and Pauline Trueblood, *The Recovery of Family Life* (New York: Harper and Brothers, 1953). Elton Trueblood, *Alternative to Futility* (New York and London: Harper and Brothers, 1948). Elton Trueblood, *Signs of Hope* (New York: Harper and Brothers, 1950). Elton Trueblood, *Your Other Vocation* (New York: Harper and Brothers, 1952). Elton Trueblood, *The Company of the Committed* (New York: Harper and Brothers, 1961).
6. Mark Gibbs and T. Ralph Morton, *God's Frozen People* (Philadelphia: Westminster, 1965).
7. Mark Gibbs and T. Ralph Morton, *God's Lively People* (Philadelphia: Westminster, 1970).
8. Martin Marty, "The Years of the Evangelicals," *Christian Century* (February 15, 1989): 171–74.
9. Robert Bellah, et al., *Habits of the Heart* (New York: Harper & Row, 1985).
10. *The Unchurched American—10 Years Later*, 3.
11. Bellah, et al., *Habits of the Heart*, 226.
12. *The Unchurched American—10 Years Later*, 3.
13. Ibid.
14. Paul Tillich, *The Dynamics of Faith* (New York: Harper & Row, 1957), ix.

15. John E. Biersdorf, *Hunger for Experience: Vital Religious Communities in America* (New York: Seabury, 1975), 136.

16. Ibid., 121.

17. Untitled news release from United Methodist News Service, Nashville, TN (March 15, 1989): 2.

18. Dr. Constance Leean, *Faith Development in the Adult Life Cycle* (New York: Religious Association Press, 1985), Module 2, 61.

19. *JSAC Grapevine*, Newsletter of Joint Strategy and Action Committee, New York (February 1989): 1.

20. No author, "The GAC's 'Vision,'" *The Presbyterian Layman*, newspaper of the Presbyterian Lay Committee, Inc., Springfield, PA (November/December 1988).

21. Bellah, et al., *Habits of the Heart*, 241.

22. Ibid., 242.

23. Ibid., 243.

24. *JSAC Grapevine*, 3.

PART II. COMPETENCY

Chapter 2. Just Doing My Job

1. Judith Valente, "Tense Touchdown," *Wall Street Journal* (March 1, 1989): 1; and "Crew Describes Saving of Damaged Jetliner," Allentown, PA, *Morning Call* (March 4, 1989): A18.

2. No author, "The Meaning of the Spiritual Life," *Initiatives*, the newsletter of the National Center for the Laity, Chicago, IL (May/June 1984): 1.

3. Gregory F. Augustine Pierce, "A Spirituality of Work," *Praying* (September-October 1983): 26.

4. William Droel and Gregory F. Augustine Pierce, *Confident and Competent* (Notre Dame, IN: Ave Maria Press, 1987), 42.

5. Ibid., 47.

6. Quoted in Herman Stuempfle, Jr., *Theological and Biblical Perspectives on the Laity* (New York: Lutheran Church in America, 1987), 12.

7. Sharon Nelson, "The Challenge to Women," *Nation's Business* (July 1990): 16.

8. Dorothy L. Sayers, *Creed or Chaos* (New York: Harcourt, Brace, 1949), 56–57.

9. The Cuomo Commission on Trade and Competitiveness, *The Cuomo Commission Report*, edited by Lee Smith (New York: Simon and Schuster, 1988), 3.

10. Ibid., 4.

11. Ibid., 15.

12. Ibid., 18.

13. Nancy J. Perry, "Saving the Schools," *Fortune* (November 7, 1988): 42.

14. Ibid., 42.

15. The Cuomo Commission on Trade and Competitiveness, *The Cuomo Commission Report*, 20.

Chapter 3. Competency and Competition

1. Two such organizations are Marketplace, 6400 Schroeder Road, PO Box 7895, Madison, WI 53707–7895; and The Navigators, PO Box 6000, Colorado Springs, CO 80934.

2. Servant Society, 900 Calle de los Amigos, D-502, Santa Barbara, CA 93105.

PART III. PRESENCE

Chapter 4. Being There for Somebody

1. Earl Koile, *Listening as a Way of Becoming* (Waco, TX: Regency Books, 1977); John Drakeford, *The Awesome Power of the Listening Ear* (Waco, TX: Word Books, 1967).
2. Susan Champlin Taylor, "A Thoughtful Word, A Healing Touch," *Modern Maturity* (January 1989): 27–29.

Chapter 5. The Need for Grace

1. Gerhard Ebeling, *Luther* (Philadelphia: Fortress, 1972), 40.

PART IV. ETHICS

Chapter 6. A Crisis in Ethics

1. Richard Stengel and David Beckwirth, "Morality Among the Supply-Siders," *Time* (May 25, 1987): 18–20.
2. Robert Wagman, "Ethics: Its Decline and Fall During the Reagan Presidency," Allentown, PA, *Morning Call* (September 4, 1988): A10.
3. Ibid.
4. Fred Wertheimer, "Window of Opportunity: The Climate Is Ripe for Ethical Reforms," *Common Cause Magazine* (July/August 1989): 45.
5. Felix G. Rohatyn, "Ethics in America's Money Culture," *New York Times* (June 3, 1987): 12.
6. From *Business Ethics Resource*, a newsletter of Revehen Consultants, Brookline, MA, edited by Judith A. Ewing.
7. Rick Wartzman, "Nature or Nurture? Study Blames Ethical Lapses on Corporate Goals," *Wall Street Journal* (October 9, 1987): 21.
8. Ibid.
9. The Trinity Center for Ethics and Corporate Policy, Trinity Church, 74 Trinity Place, New York, NY 10006.
10. The Center for Ethics and Corporate Policy, 637 South Dearborn, Chicago, IL 60605.
11. Interfaith Center on Corporate Responsibility, 475 Riverside Drive, Room 566, New York, NY 10115.

Chapter 7. Decisions, Decisions!

1. No author, *Life in All Its Fullness: The Word of God and Human Rights* (New York: American Bible Society and the Human Rights Office of the National Council of Churches of Christ in the USA, 1976).
2. Ibid., 55.
3. Ibid.

4. Ibid., 69.

5. David Wessel, "Overall Poverty Rate Nearly Flat in '87, But Levels for Blacks Rose Substantially," *Wall Street Journal* (September 1, 1988): 21.

6. Ibid.

7. *Life in All Its Fullness: The Word of God and Human Rights*, 56.

8. Ibid.

9. Manuel G. Velasquez, *Business Ethics* (Englewood Cliffs, NJ: Prentice-Hall, 1988), 99–106.

10. "Economic Justice: Stewardship of Creation in Human Community," Social Statement of the Lutheran Church in America, 231 Madison Avenue, New York, 1980.

11. David Gibson, ed., "Economic Justice for All: Catholic Social Teaching and the US Economy," *Origins, NC Documentary Service* (June 5, 1986). National Catholic News Service, 1312 Massachusetts Ave. NW, Washington, DC. ISSN 0093–609X.

12. Audrey Chapman Smock, ed., "Christian Faith and Economic Life," United Church Board for World Ministries, 475 Riverside Drive, New York, NY 10115, 1987.

13. "Christian Faith and Economic Justice," Presbyterian Church (USA), 100 Witherspoon St., Louisville, KY 40202.

14. "Economic Justice for All," 1.

15. Velasquez, *Business Ethics*, 114.

16. Ibid.

PART V. CHANGE

Chapter 8. The Courage to Change

1. Thomas J. Peters and Robert H. Waterman, Jr., *In Search of Excellence: Lessons from America's Best-Run Companies* (New York: Harper & Row, 1982), 122.

2. Veronica Zundel, comp., *Eerdmans' Book of Famous Prayers* (Grand Rapids: William B. Eerdmans, 1983), 87.

3. Kenneth R. Clark, "Tigress of the Tube," *Chicago Tribune* (March 12, 1989).

4. Lyle E. Schaller, *The Change Agent* (Nashville: Abingdon Press, 1972), 81.

5. Richard J. Foster, *Money, Sex and Power* (San Francisco: Harper & Row, 1985), 227.

6. Reinhold Niebuhr, *Moral Man and Immoral Society* (New York: Charles Scribner's Sons, 1932).

7. William Stringfellow, *An Ethic for Christians and Other Aliens in a Strange Land* (Waco, TX: Word Books, 1973), 78.

8. Jaclyn Fierman,"Why Women Still Don't Hit the Top," *Fortune* (July 30, 1990): 40.

9. Ibid., 42.

Chapter 9. Bringing About Change

1. William Droel and Gregory F. Augustine Pierce, *Confident and Competent* (Notre Dame, IN: Ave Maria Press, 1987), 57.

2. Miriam Pawel, "Cuomo Dispenses Ecumenical Advice," *Newsday* (May 20, 1985): 17.

3. William Diehl, *God's Agents for Change* (Philadelphia: Parish Life Press, 1983).

4. There are specific times and procedures to follow in filing shareholder resolutions. A phone call or letter to the Investor Responsibility Research Center, Inc., 1755 Massachusetts Ave., Washington, DC 20036 will provide details on how to proceed.

PART VI. LIFE-STYLE

Chapter 10. The Need to Give

1. Don Oldenburg, "One Thing You Can Trust, Cynicism Is More Pervasive Than Ever in US," *Washington Post*, reprinted in the Allentown, PA *Morning Call* (June 29, 1989): D1.
2. Ibid.
3. Ronald Henkoff, "Is Greed Dead?" *Fortune* (August 14, 1989): 40–49.
4. Ibid., 41.
5. Virginia A. Hodgkinson and Murray S. Weitzman, *Giving and Volunteering in the United States: Summary of Findings* (Washington, DC: Independent Sector, 1988).
6. Virginia A. Hodgkinson and Murray S. Weitzman, *The Charitable Behavior of Americans: A National Survey* (Washington, DC: Independent Sector and The Rockefeller Brothers Fund, 1986).
7. No author, *Daring Goals for a Caring Society: A Blueprint for Substantial Giving and Volunteering in America* (Washington, DC: Independent Sector, 1986).
8. Laurence Urdang, editor in chief, *The Random House Dictionary of the English Language* (New York: Random House, 1968).
9. *Daring Goals for a Caring Society*, 3.

Chapter 11. Living on the Low Side

1. Martin Luther, *The Large Catechism of Martin Luther* (Philadelphia: Fortress Press, 1959), 9.
2. Donella Meadows, et al., *The Limits to Growth* (New York: Universe Books, 1972), 56–59.
3. Charles McCoy, "Thriving Thrift," *Wall Street Journal* (June 29, 1990).
4. Richard Foster, *Celebration of Discipline* (San Francisco: Harper & Row, 1978), 74.
5. Shawn Tully, "American Bosses are Overpaid," *Fortune* (November 7, 1988): 121–36.
6. Ibid., 124.
7. Ibid., 136.
8. "Careers Count Most for the Well-To-Do," *Wall Street Journal* (October 16, 1989).
9. Hodgkinson and Weitzman, *Giving and Volunteering in the United States: Summary of Findings*, 22.
10. Subrata N. Chakravarty and Katherine Weisman, "Consuming Our Children?" *Forbes* (November 14, 1988): 222–32.
11. Ibid.
12. Ibid.
13. Susan B. Garland and Pat Houston, "Suddenly, It's 'The Year of the Child.'" *Business Week* (April 4, 1988): 36.

PART VII. MAKING THE CONNECTION

Chapter 12. Roles and Responsibilities

1. "No Need to Ask," editorial, *The Catholic Messenger*, Davenport, IA (March 17, 1988): 8.
2. Frank W. Klos, "Report on the Ecumenical Consultation, New Trends in Laity Formation, Assisi (Italy), September 7–17, 1974," report to the Lutheran Church in America, New York.
3. Hendrik Kraemer, *A Theology of the Laity* (London: Lutterworth Press, 1958), 26.
4. Ibid., 30.
5. Second Vatican Council, *Dogmatic Constitution on the Church, Lumen Gentium*.
6. Ibid., 57.
7. Ibid., 57, 58.
8. Ibid., 63.
9. "A Chicago Declaration of Christian Concern." Copies of this statement can be secured through the National Center for the Laity, 1 East Superior St., Chicago, IL 60611.
10. Ibid.
11. Ibid.
12. The National Center for the Laity, 1 East Superior St., Chicago, IL 60611.
13. *Canon III.1* of the Episcopal Church, 815 Second Ave., New York, NY 10017.
14. "The Ministry of the Whole People of God; Living Our Faith Where We Are," Statement of Concern adopted at the 1987 Biennial Meeting of the American Baptist Churches of the USA, PO Box 851, Valley Forge, PA 19482–0851.
15. *Book of Discipline*, The United Methodist Church, PO Box 840, Nashville, TN 37202; Pronouncement on "Empowering the Laity for Ministry" adopted at the 1981 General Synod of the United Church of Christ, 1400 N. Seventh St., St. Louis, MO 63106–4545; "The Ministry of the Laity: A Foundational Paper," adopted by the Southern Baptist Convention Coordinating Committee, 1350 Spring St. NW, Atlanta, GA 30367; "Declaration of Ministry," adopted by the former Lutheran Church in America. Copies can be secured through the Division for Ministry, Evangelical Lutheran Church in America, 8765 W. Higgins Road, Chicago, IL 60631.
16. Kraemer, *A Theology of the Laity*, 62.
17. Ibid., 72.
18. See note 14, above.
19. William E. Diehl, *In Search of Faithfulness* (Philadelphia: Fortress, 1987).
20. Evaluation report on the "Faith in Daily Life" project of Auburn Seminary, July 1989, Auburn Theological Seminary, 3041 Broadway, New York, NY 10027.
21. Ibid.
22. For detailed information write to the Division for Congregational Life, Evangelical Lutheran Church in America, 8765 W. Higgins Road, Chicago, IL 60631.
23. *Laity Exchange*, 311 MacArthur Blvd., San Leandro, CA 94577; *Centering*, the Center for the Ministry of the Laity, 210 Herrick Road, Newton Center, MA 62159; *Lay Communiqueé*, the Alban Institute, 4125 Nebraska Ave. NW, Washington, DC 20016.
24. No author, *The Unchurched American—10 Years Later* (Princeton, NJ: Princeton Research Center, 1988).

Bibliography

Banks, Robert. *All the Business of Life: Bringing Theology Down to Earth* (Claremont, CA: Albatross Books, 1987). Practical ways to connect our beliefs with the activities of daily life.

Crabtree, Davida Foy. *The Empowering Church* (Washington, DC: The Alban Institute, 1989). A very creative pastor tells how her congregation supports the ministries of its people in the world.

Droel, William and Gregory F. Augustine Pierce. *Confident and Competent: A Challenge for the Lay Church* (Notre Dame, IN: Ave Maria Press, 1987). How to bring spirituality into work—a fresh approach.

Foster, Richard J. *Freedom of Simplicity* (New York: Harper & Row, 1981). How to live in simple harmony with the many complexities of life.

Franke, Merle G. *Lord, Where Are You? I'm Hip Deep in Alligators* (Lima, OH: C.S.S. Publishing Company, 1985). A small book of prayer reflections for people in the business community.

Gibbs, Mark. *Christians with Secular Power* (Philadelphia: Fortress Press, 1981). A thoughtful book for those who are called to wield secular power.

Hardy, Lee. *The Fabric of this World: Inquiries Into Calling, Career Choice and the Design of Human Work* (Grand Rapids: William B. Eerdmans, 1990). How the Protestant Reformation brought a new sense of religious dignity to work, and how the proper understanding of vocation can shape one's outlook on career.

Haugk, Kenneth C. *Christian Caregiving: A Way of Life* (Minneapolis: Augsburg Press, 1984). Practical ways in which to bring God's presence into our relationships with others.

Johnson, Paul G. *Grace: God's Work Ethic* (Valley Forge: Judson Press, 1985). Bringing the gospel of God's grace into the weekday world of works.

Mahedy, William and Christopher Carstens. *Starting on Monday: Christian Living in the Workplace* (New York: Ballantine Books, 1987). How to identify the moral issues in our lives and how to relate our faith to them.

Raines, John C. and Donna C. Day-Lower. *Modern Work and Human Meaning* (Philadelphia: Westminster Press, 1986). Considers work from the perspective of blue-collar workers, women, and the poor.

Rowthorn, Anne. *The Liberation of the Laity* (Wilton, CT: Morehouse-Barlow, 1986). An impassioned plea for the church to liberate its laity for ministry in the world.

Tucker, Graham. *The Faith-Work Connection: A Practical Application of Christian Values in the Marketplace* (Toronto, Canada: Anglican Book Centre, 1987). How to integrate Christian principles into management styles.

Vos, Nelvin. *Seven Days a Week: Faith in Action* (Philadelphia: Fortress Press, 1985). Taking our faith into the arenas of family, occupation, leisure, community, and church.

Wingeier, Douglas E. *Working Out Your Own Beliefs: A Guide for Doing Your Own Theology* (Nashville: Abingdon Press, 1980). How to use the resources of Scripture and Christian tradition to "do" theology in the experiences of daily life.